FOR ORGANS, PIANOS & ELECTRONIC KEYBOARDS

E-Z PLAY TODAY

358

Gospel Songs of Hank Williams

T004113Y

CONTENTS

ISBN 0-634-00697-5

HAL•LEONARD®
CORPORATION

7777 W. BLUEMOUND RD. P.O. BOX 13819 MILWAUKEE, WI 53213

Visit Hal Leonard Online at
www.halleonard.com

Angel of Death

Registration 2
Rhythm: Waltz

Words and Music by
Hank Williams

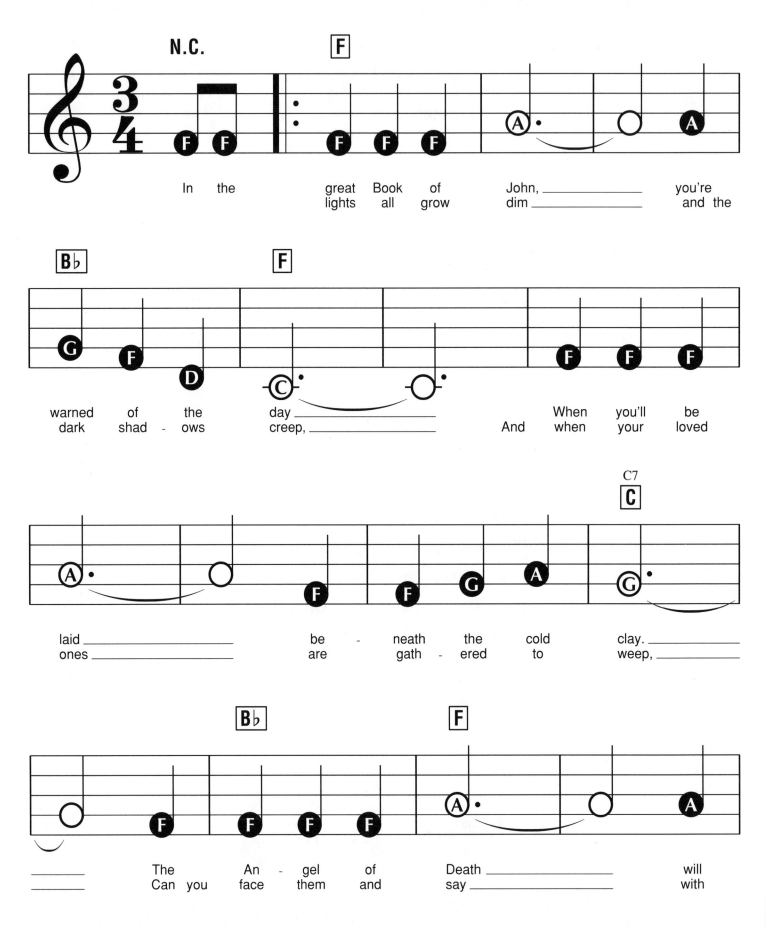

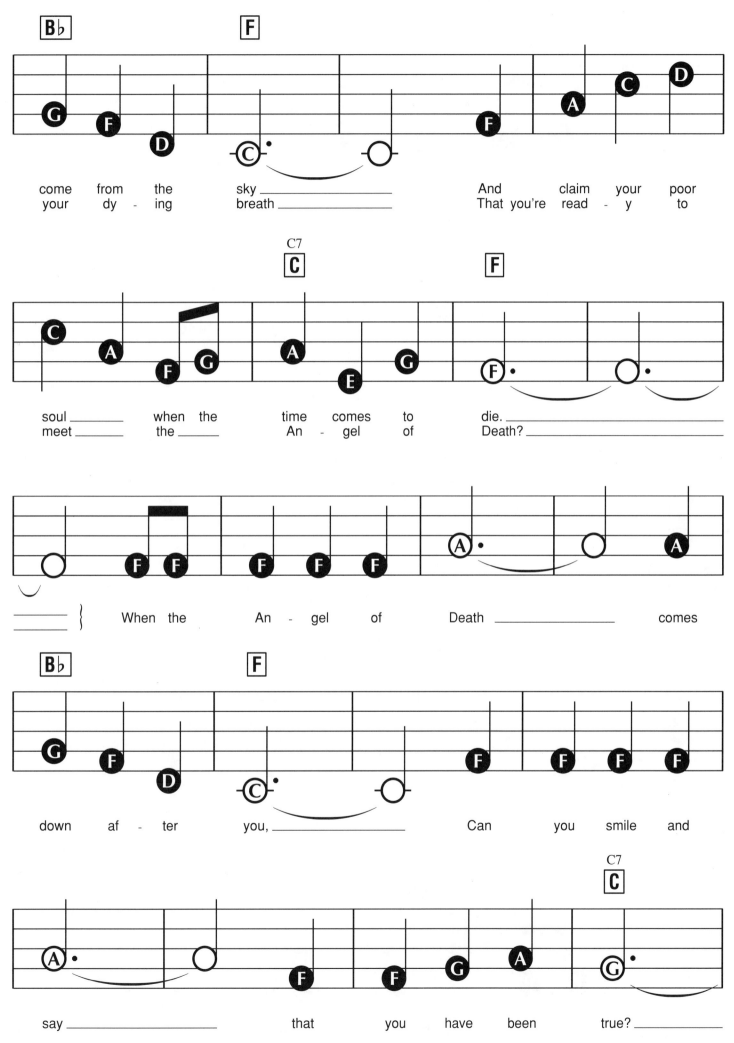

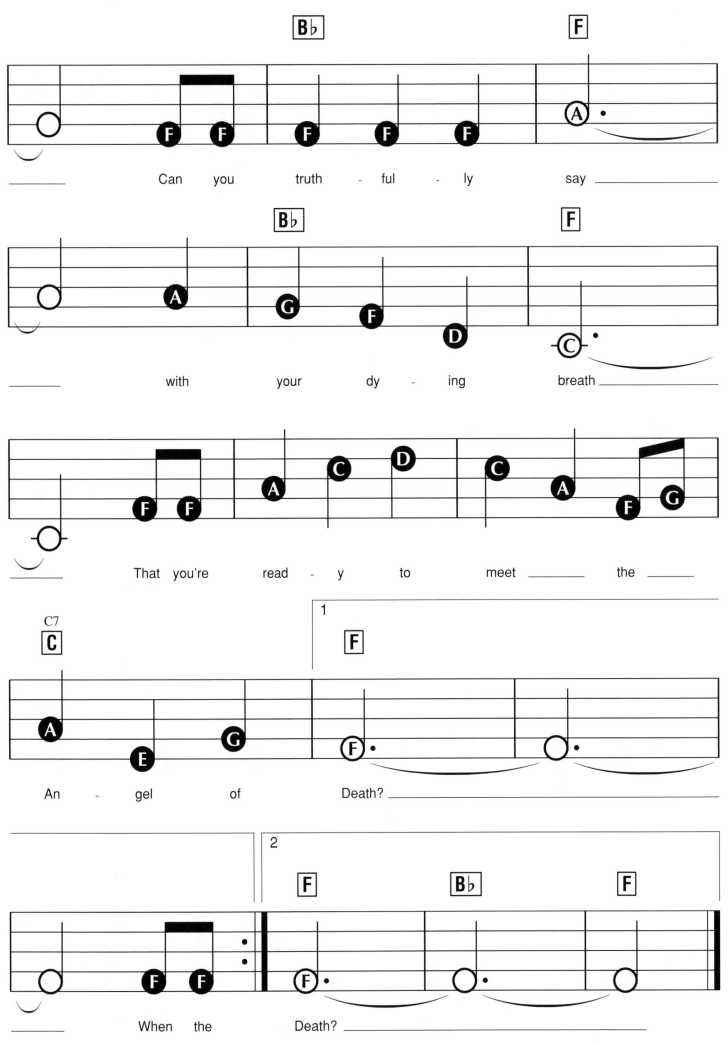

Are You Walkin' and A-Talkin' for the Lord

Registration 4
Rhythm: Fox Trot or Country

Words and Music by
Hank Williams

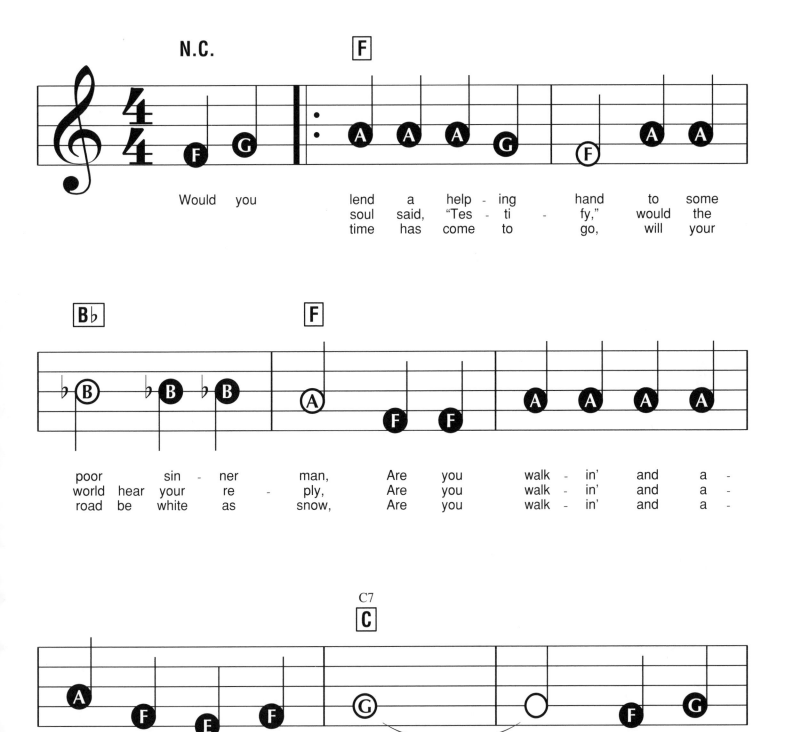

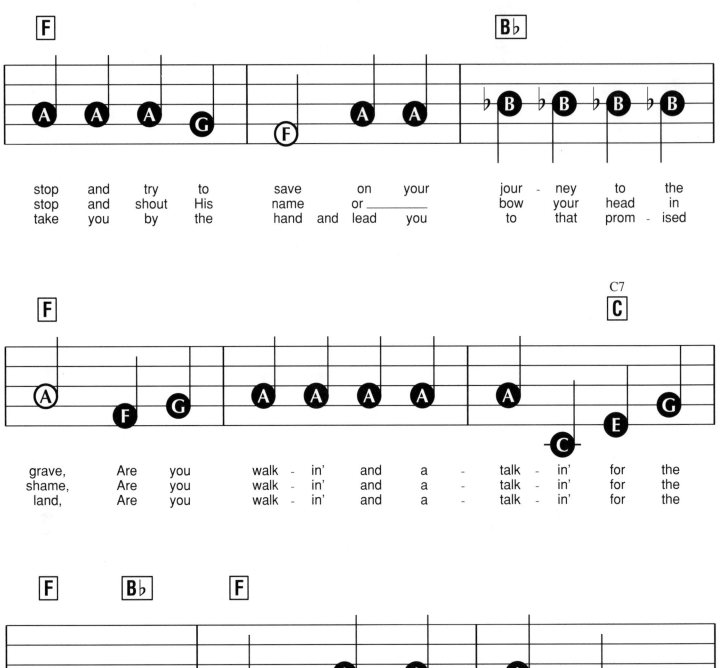

stop and try to save on your jour - ney to the
stop and shout His name or _____ bow your to head in
take you by the hand and lead you to that prom - ised

grave, Are you walk - in' and a - talk - in' for the
shame, Are you walk - in' and a - talk - in' for the
land, Are you walk - in' and a - talk - in' for the

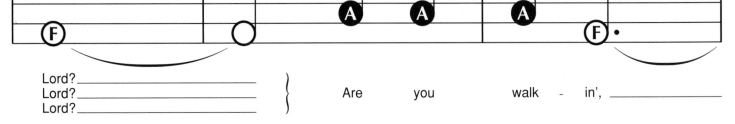

Lord? _____
Lord? _____   Are you walk - in', _____
Lord? _____

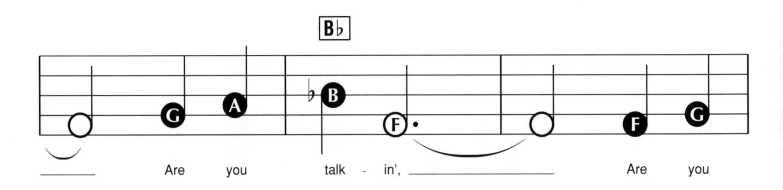

_____ Are you talk - in', _____ Are you

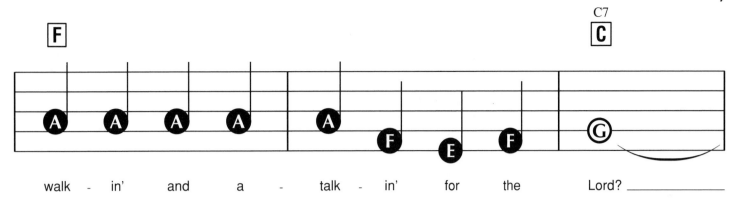

walk - in' and a - talk - in' for the Lord? _____

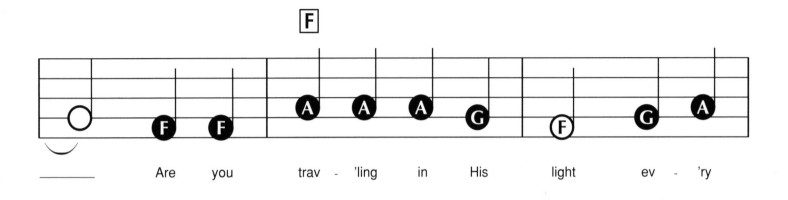

_____ Are you trav - 'ling in His light ev - 'ry

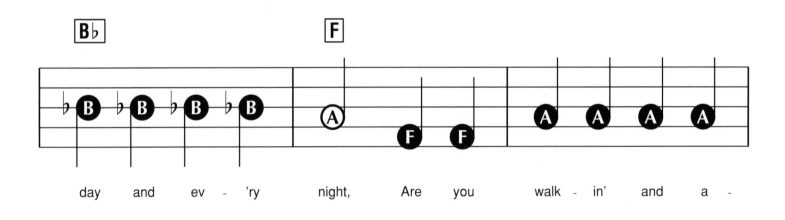

day and ev - 'ry night, Are you walk - in' and a -

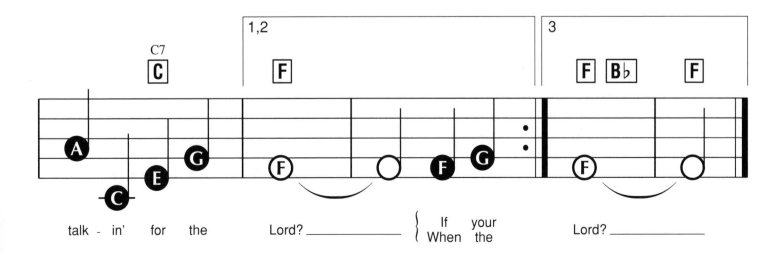

talk - in' for the Lord? _____ { If your / When the   Lord? _____

Dear Brother

Registration 10
Rhythm: Waltz

Words and Music by
Hank Williams

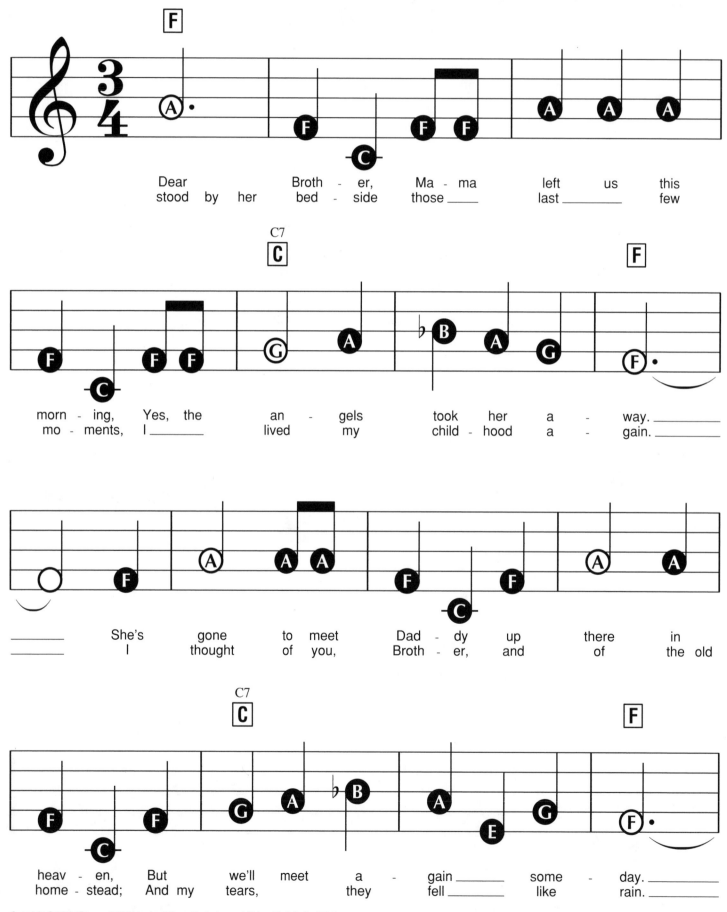

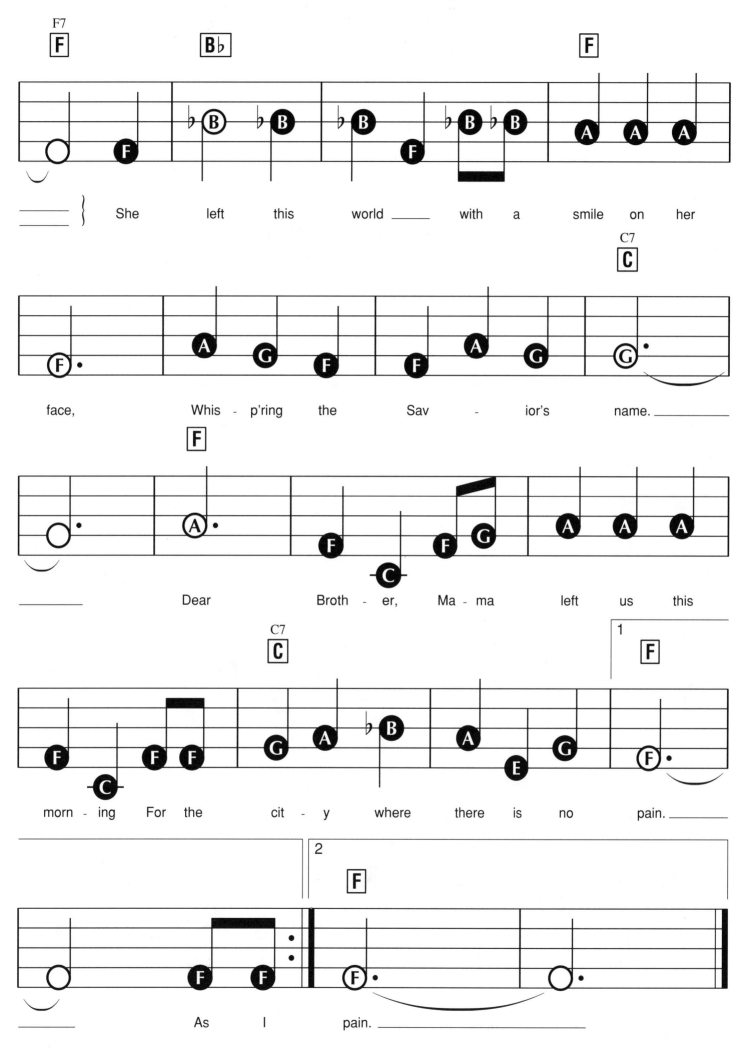

Help Me Understand

Registration 2
Rhythm: Waltz

Words and Music by
Hank Williams

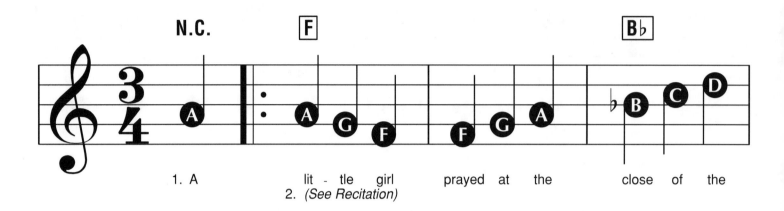

1. A lit - tle girl prayed at the close of the
2. *(See Recitation)*

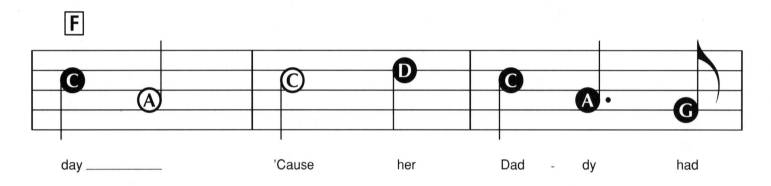

day _____ 'Cause her Dad - dy had

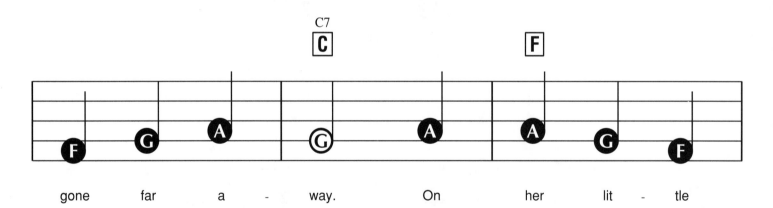

gone far a - way. On her lit - tle

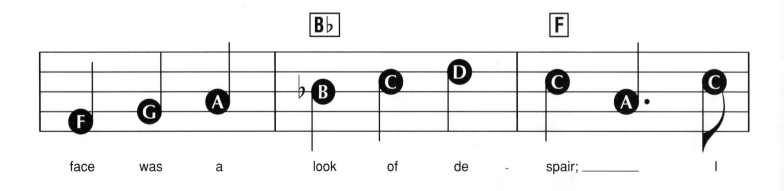

face was a look of de - spair; _____ I

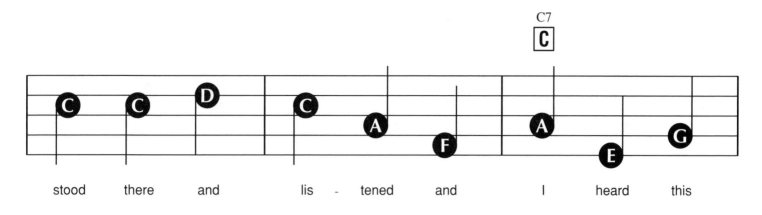

stood there and lis - tened and I heard this

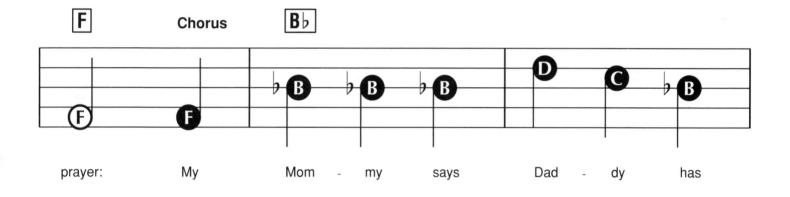

prayer: My Mom - my says Dad - dy has

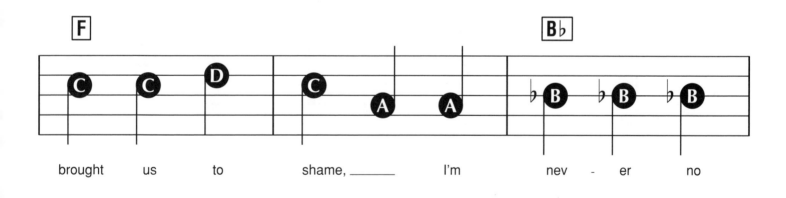

brought us to shame, _____ I'm nev - er no

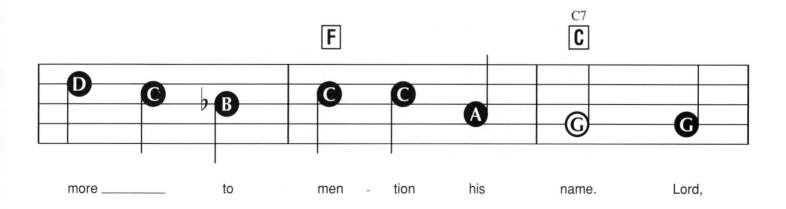

more _____ to men - tion his name. Lord,

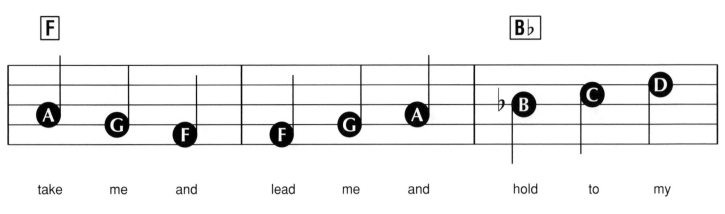

take me and lead me and hold to my

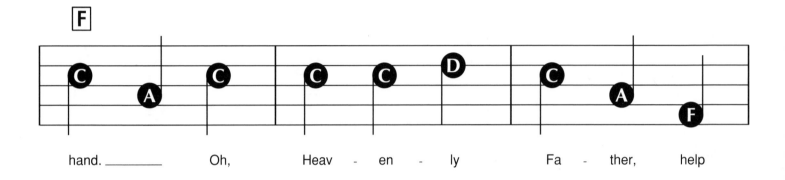

hand. _____ Oh, Heav - en - ly Fa - ther, help

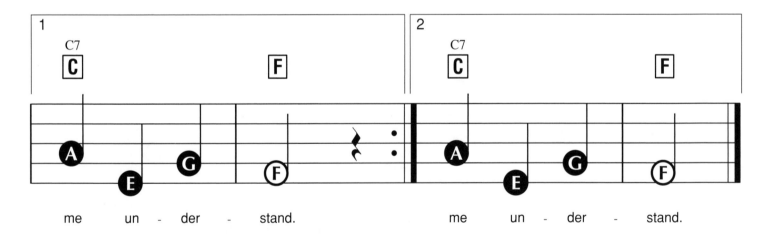

me un - der - stand.   me un - der - stand.

Recitation

You know, Friends, I wonder how many homes are broken tonight - just how many tears are shed
By some little word of anger that never should have been said.
I'd like to tell you a story of a family I once knew.
We'll call them Mary and William and their little daughter, Sue.
Mary was just a plain Mother, and Bill - well, he was the usual Dad,
And they had their family quarrels, like everyone else - but neither one got mad.
Then one day something happened - it was nothing, of course,
But one word led to another, and the last word led to a divorce.

Now here were two grown up people who failed to see common sense.
They strengthened their own selfish pride - at little Sue's expense.
You know, she didn't ask to be brought into this world - to drift from pillar to post,
But a divorce never stops to consider the one it hurts the most.
There'd be a lot more honest lovin' in this wicked world today
If just a few parted parents could hear little Sue say:
Chorus

How Can You Refuse Him Now

Registration 3
Rhythm: Waltz

Words and Music by
Hank Williams

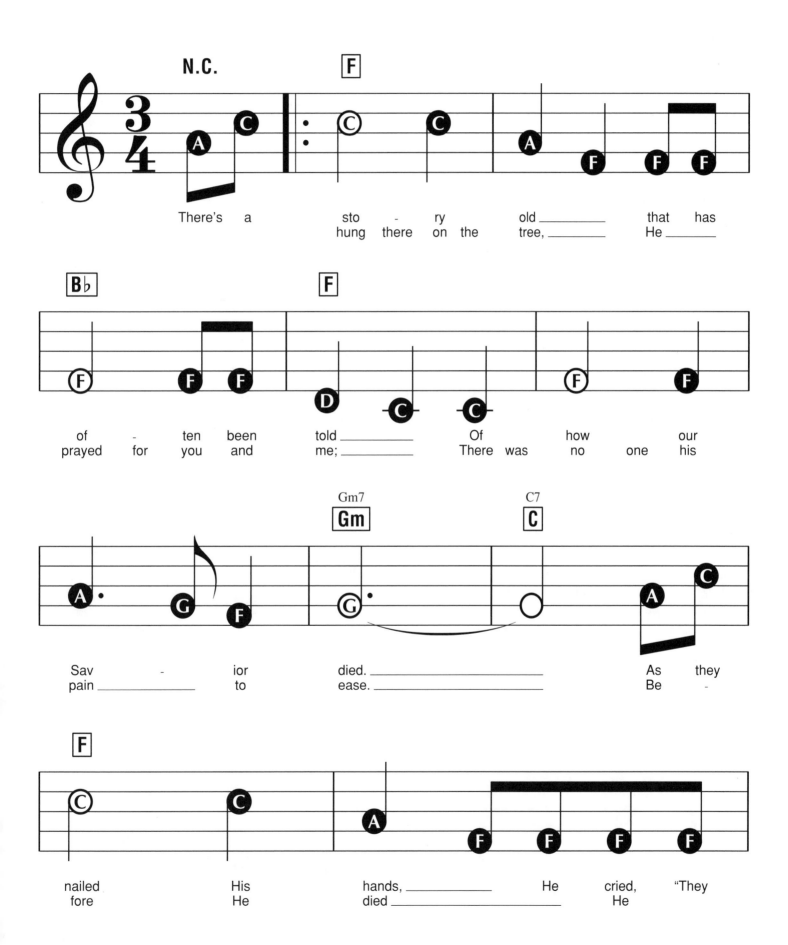

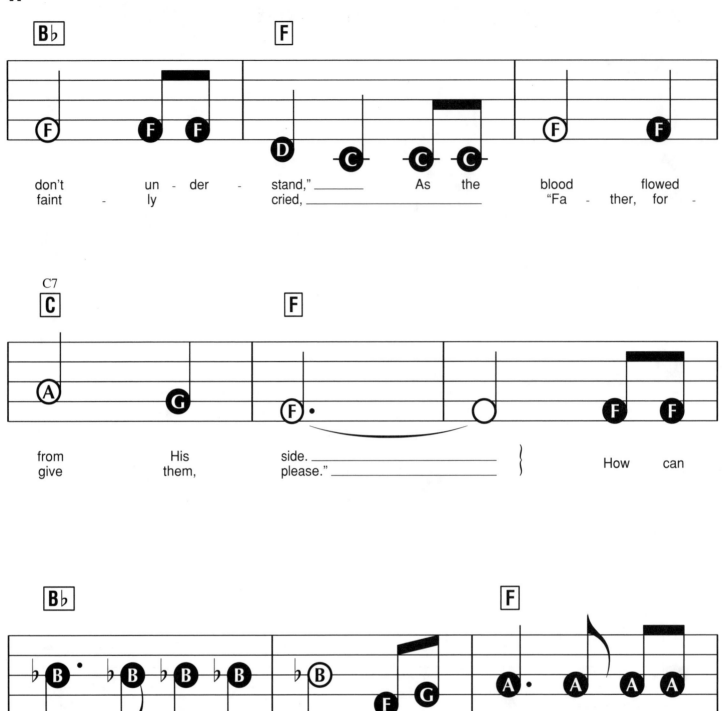

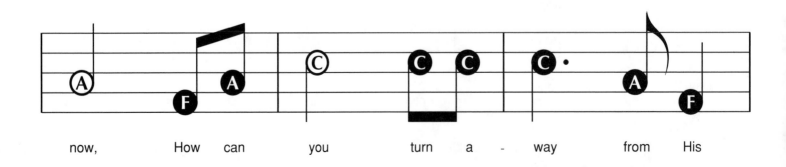

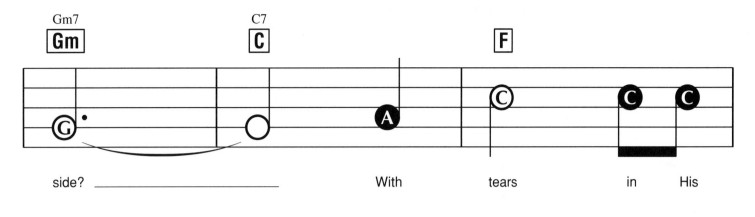

side? _____ With tears in His

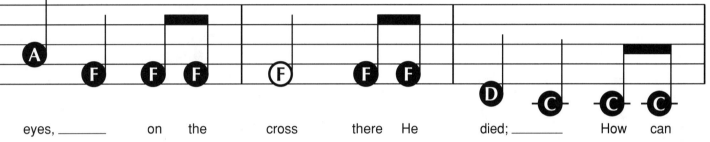

eyes, _____ on the cross there He died; _____ How can

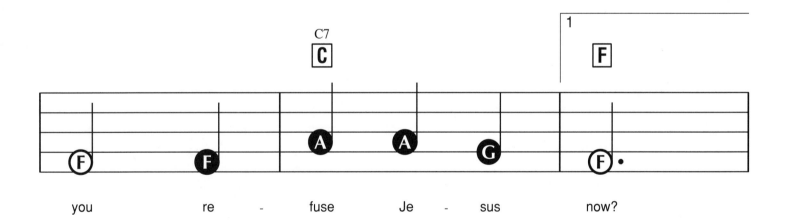

you re - fuse Je - sus now?

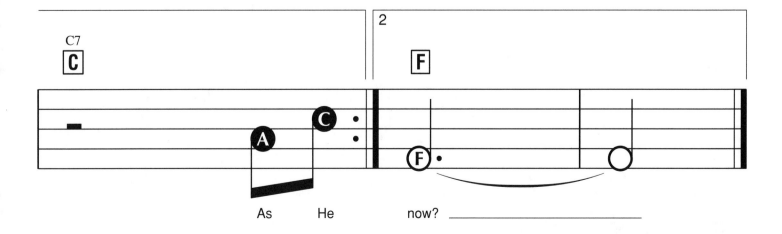

As He now? _____

A Home in Heaven

Registration 2
Rhythm: Waltz

Words and Music by
Hank Williams

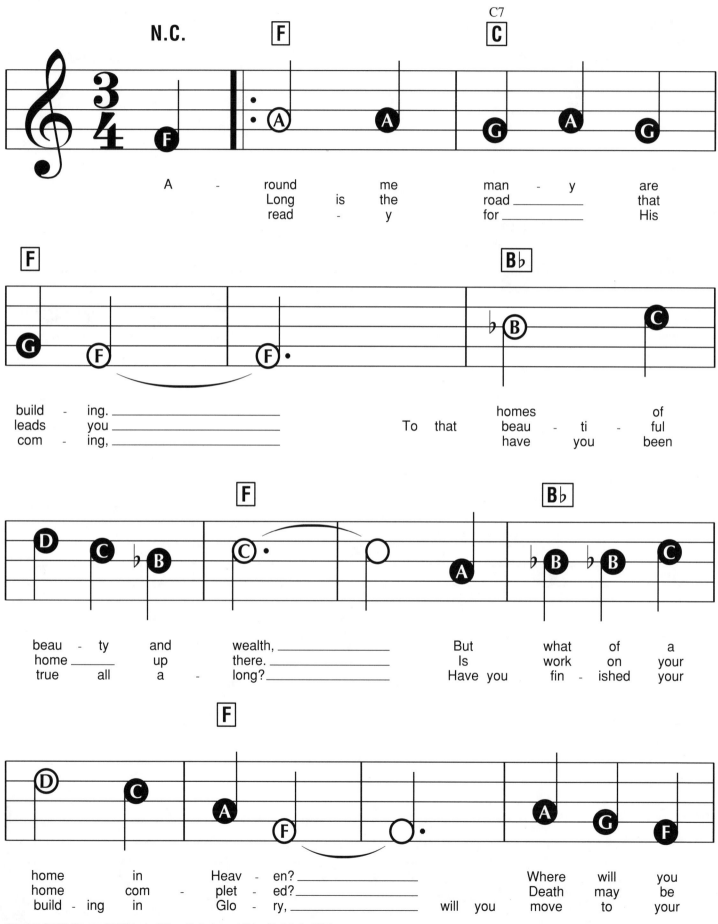

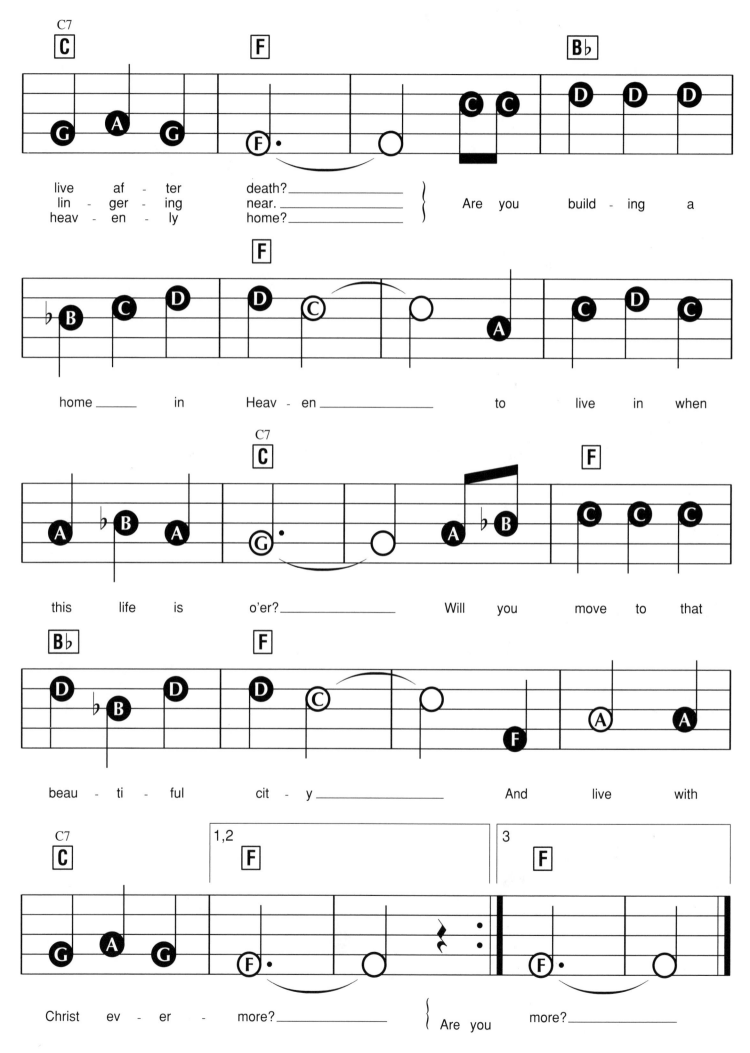

House of Gold

Registration 9
Rhythm: Country or Fox Trot

Words and Music by
Hank Williams

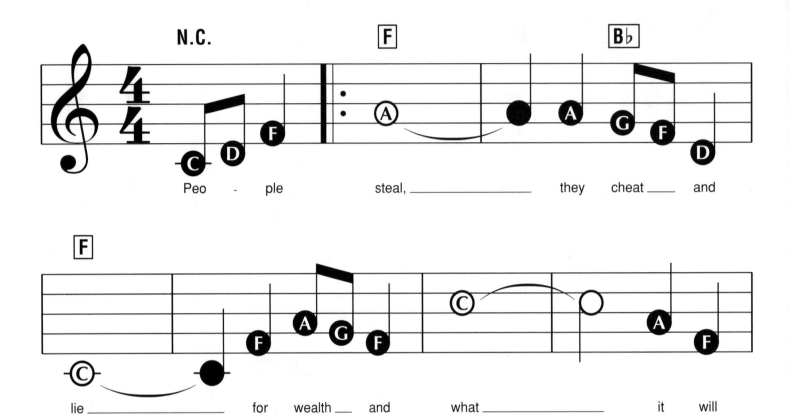

Peo - ple   steal, _____ they cheat ___ and

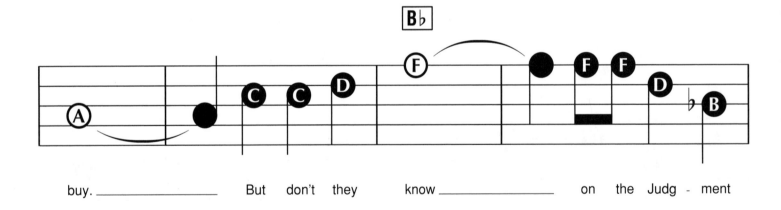

lie _____ for wealth ___ and   what _____ it will

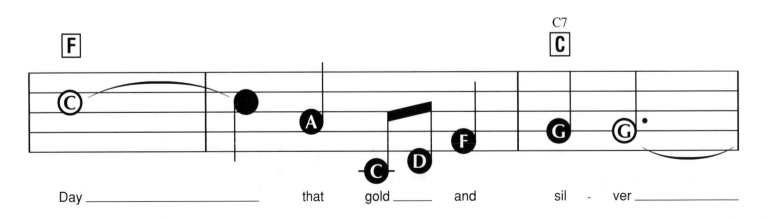

buy. _____ But don't they   know _____ on the Judg - ment

Day _____ that gold ___ and   sil - ver _____

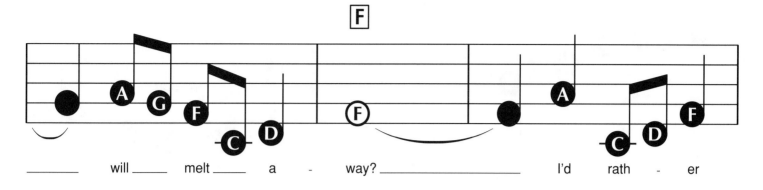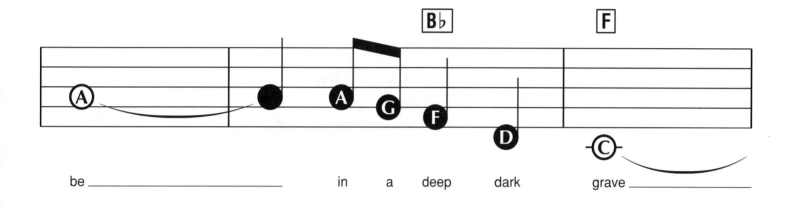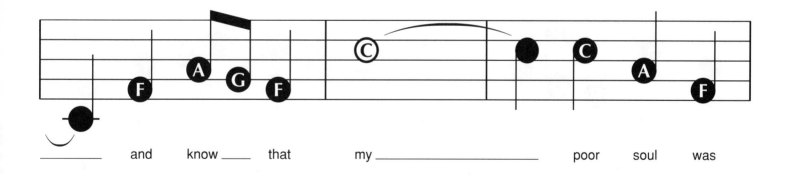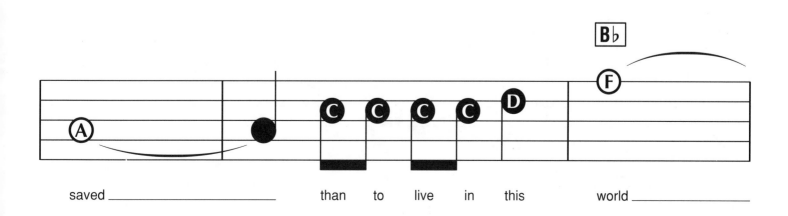

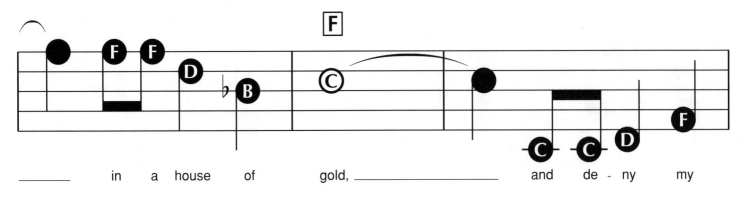

in a house of gold, _____ and de - ny my

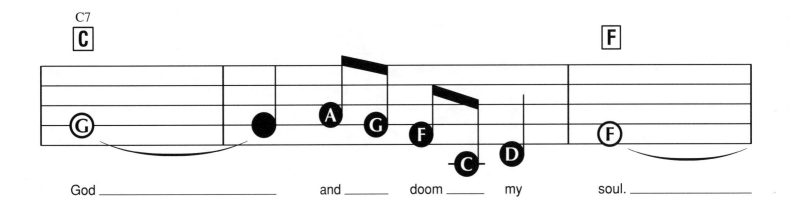

God _____ and ____ doom ____ my soul. _____

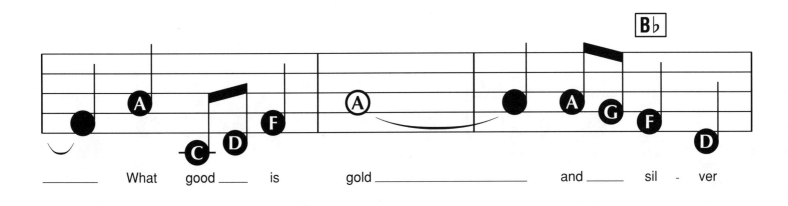

_____ What good ___ is gold _____ and ___ sil - ver

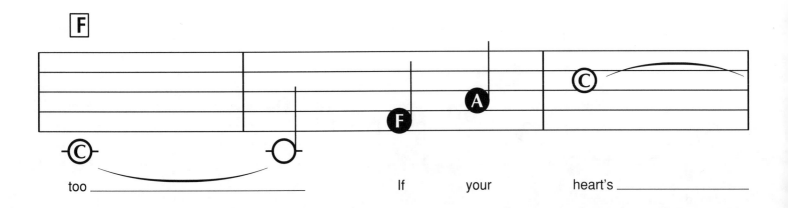

too _____ If your heart's _____

21

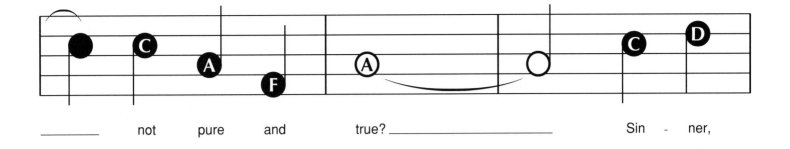

_____ not pure and true? _____ Sin - ner,

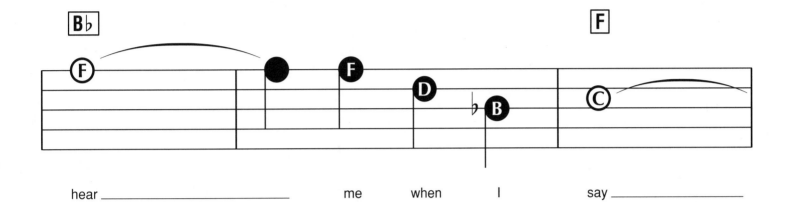

hear _____ me when I say _____

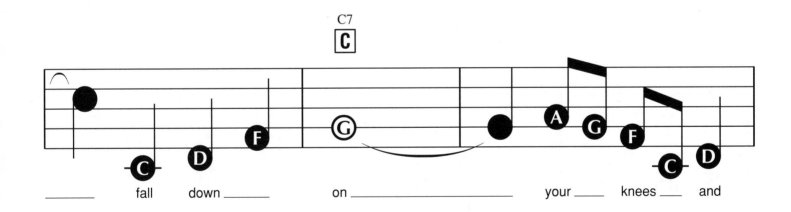

_____ fall down _____ on _____ your ____ knees ____ and

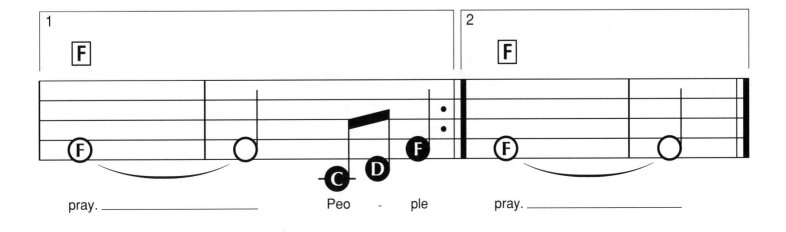

pray. _____ Peo - ple pray. _____

I Saw the Light

Registration 4
Rhythm: Fox Trot or Country

Words and Music by
Hank Williams

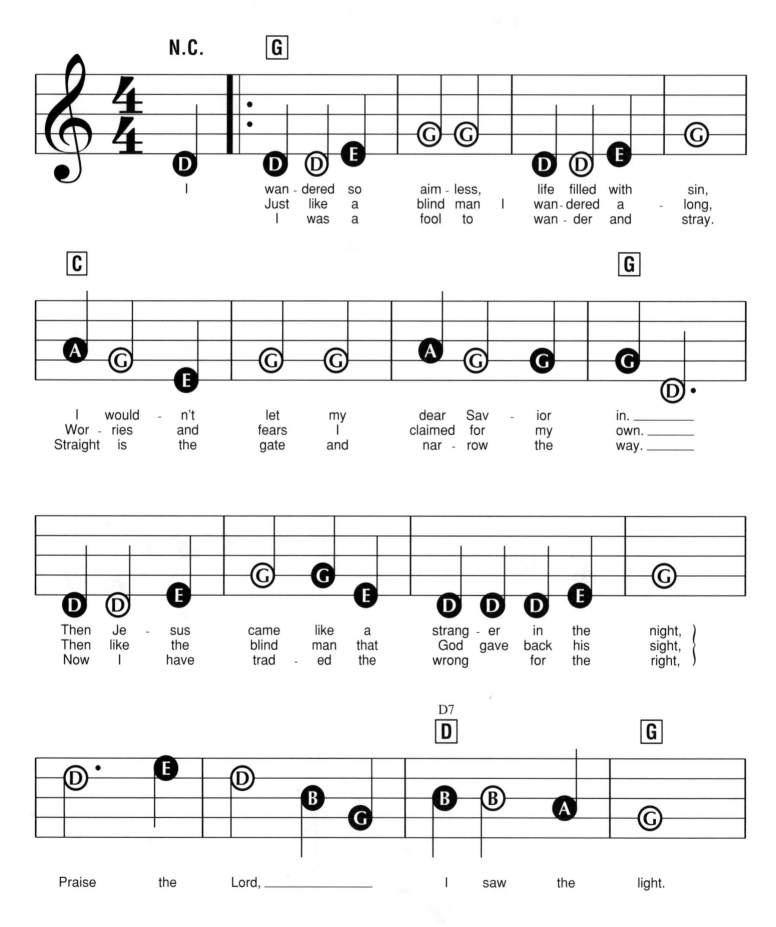

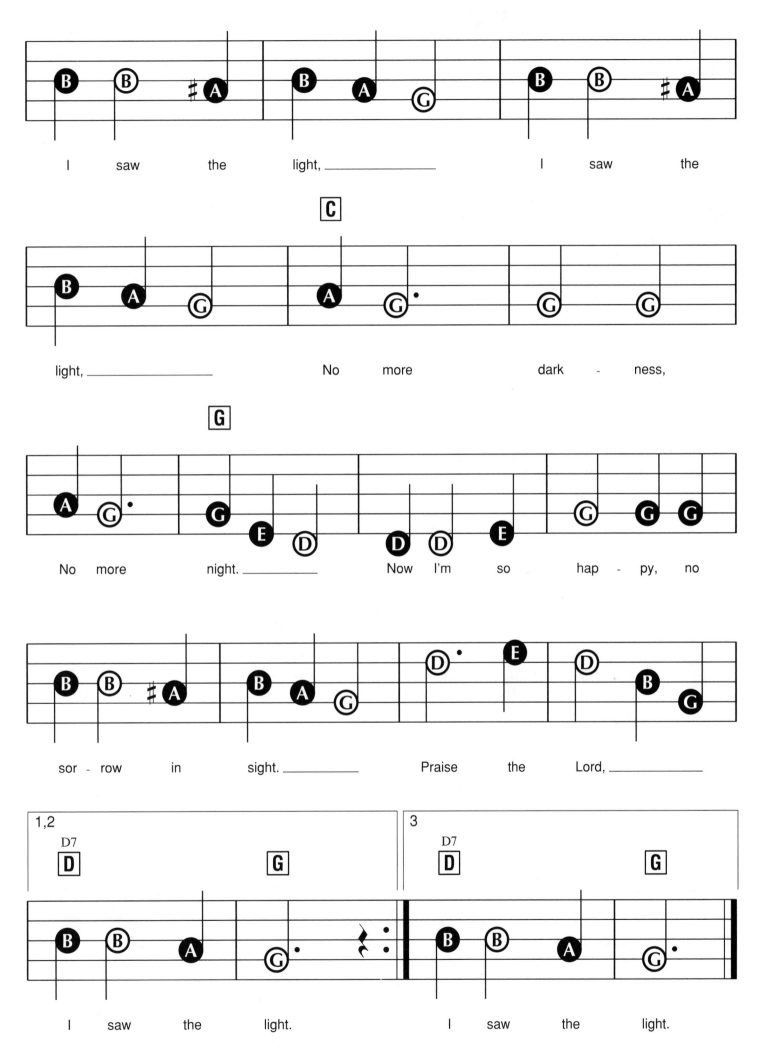

23

Jesus Died for Me

Registration 9
Rhythm: Country

Words and Music by
Hank Williams

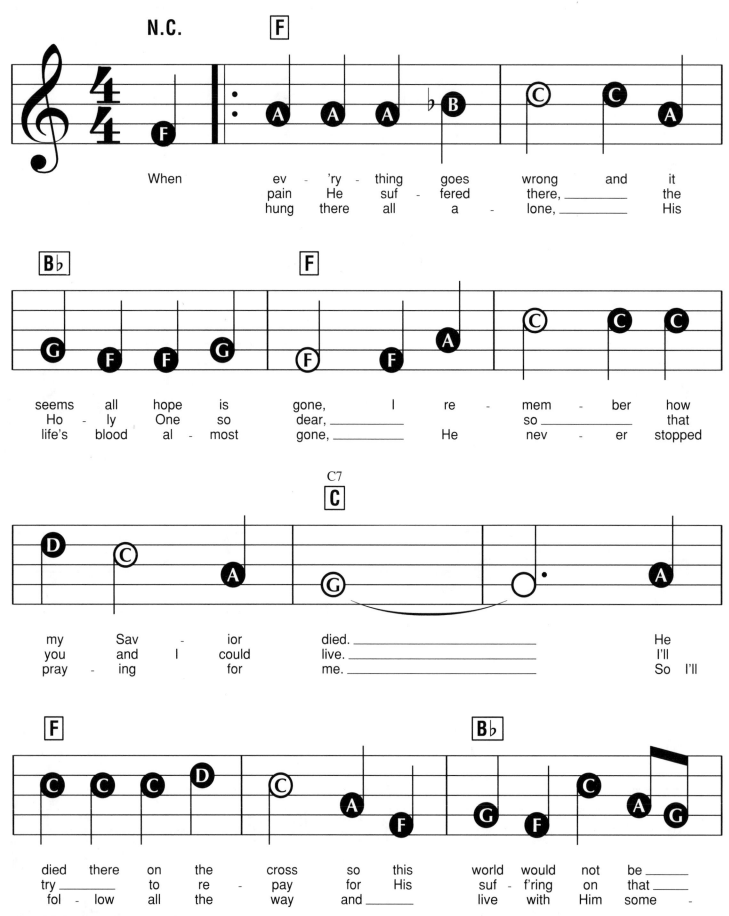

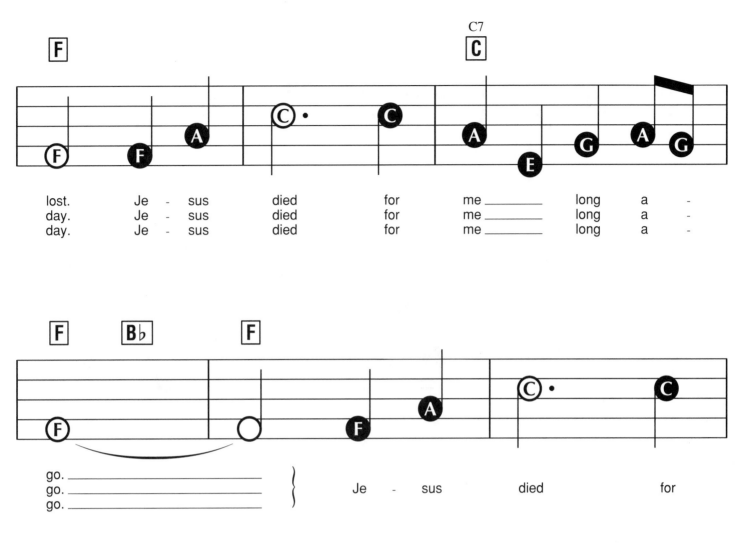

lost. Je - sus died for me _____ long a -
day. Je - sus died for me _____ long a -
day. Je - sus died for me _____ long a -

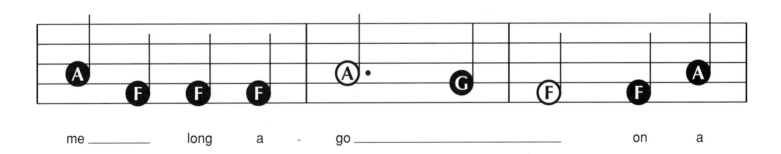

go. _____ Je - sus died for
go. _____
go. _____

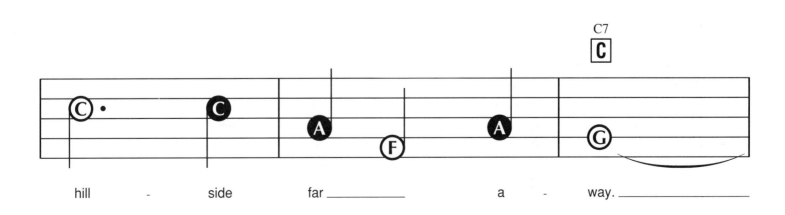

me _____ long a - go _____ on a

hill - side far _____ a - way. _____

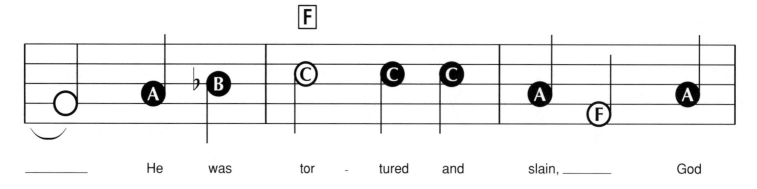

He was tor - tured and slain, _____ God

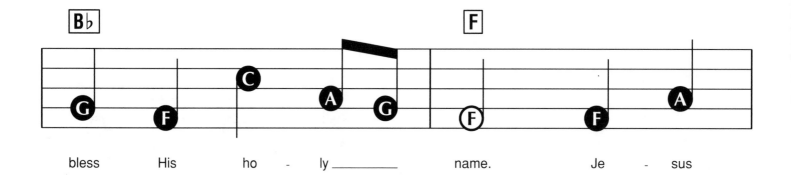

bless His ho - ly _____ name. Je - sus

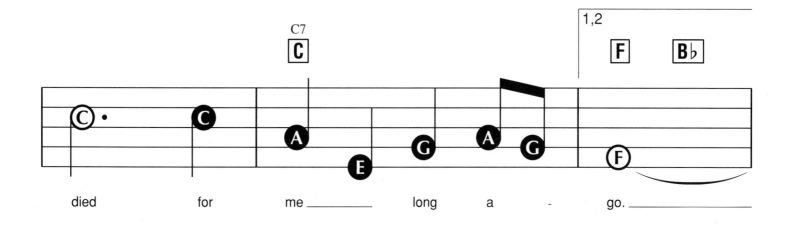

died for me _____ long a - go. _____

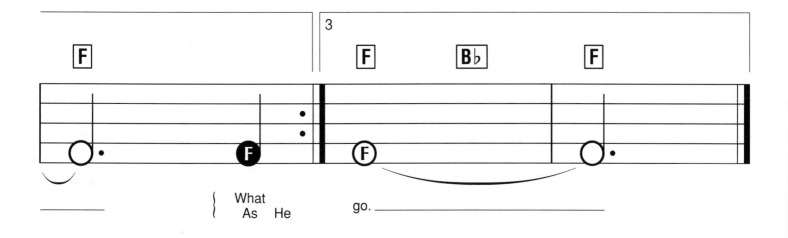

_____   { What   go. _____
             { As He

Last Night I Dreamed of Heaven

Registration 9
Rhythm: Country or Fox Trot

Words and Music by
Hank Williams

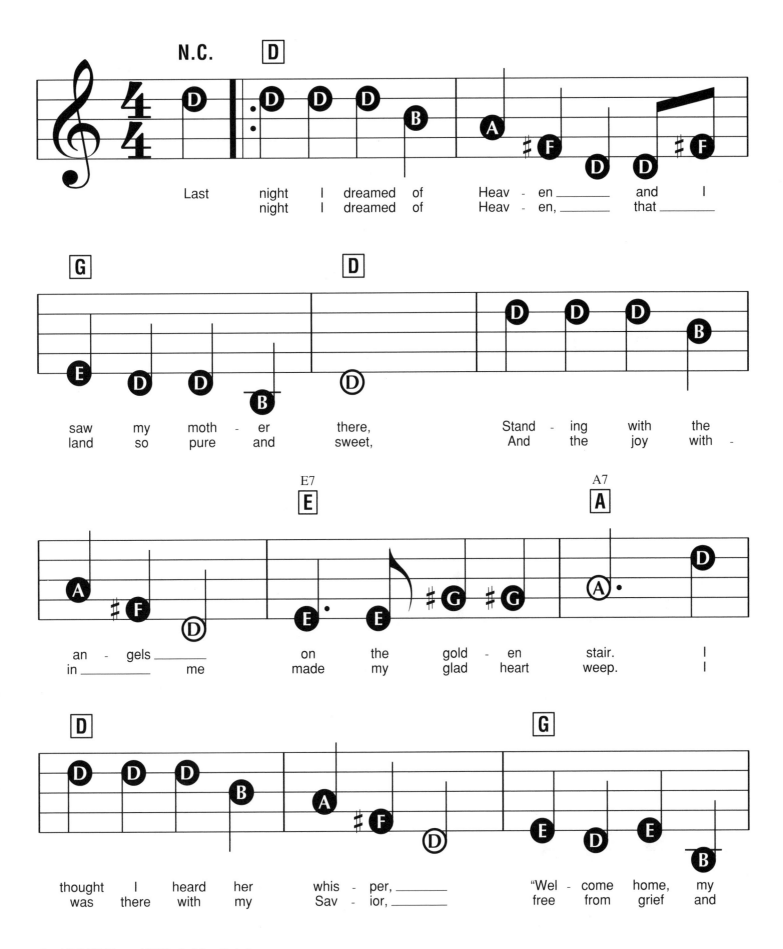

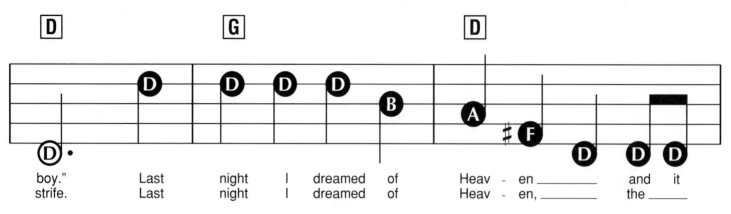

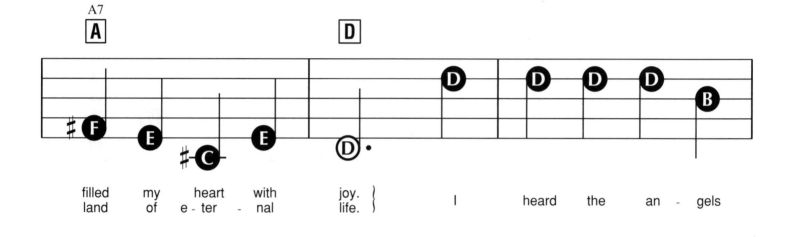

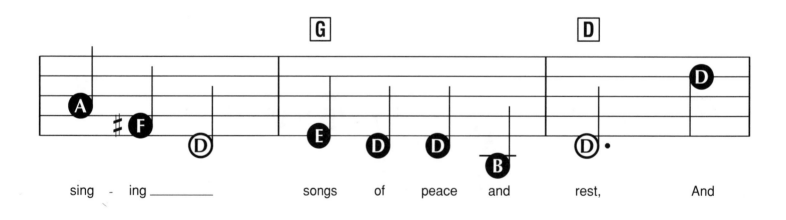

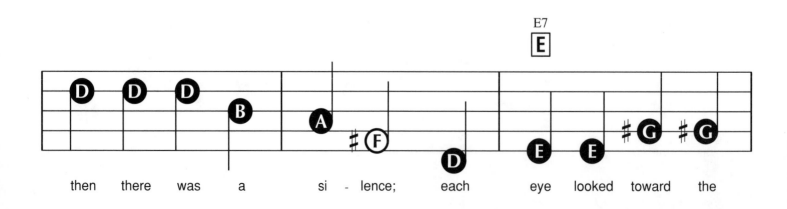

29

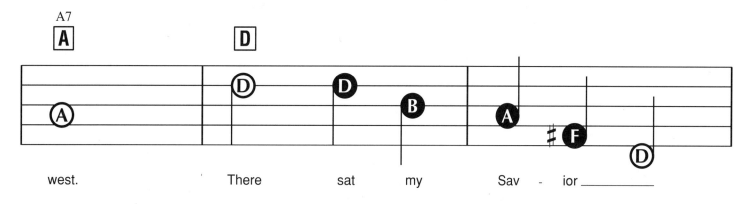

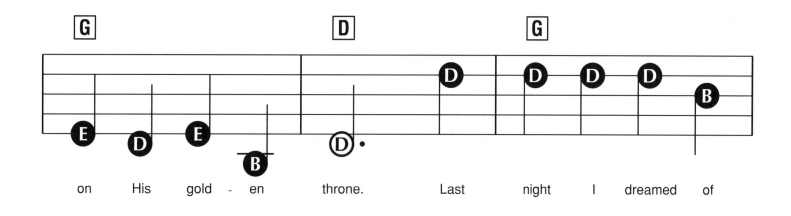

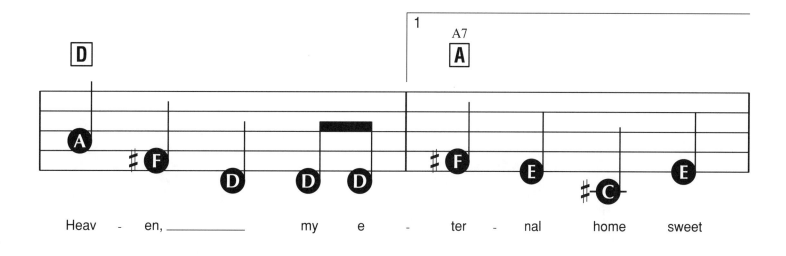

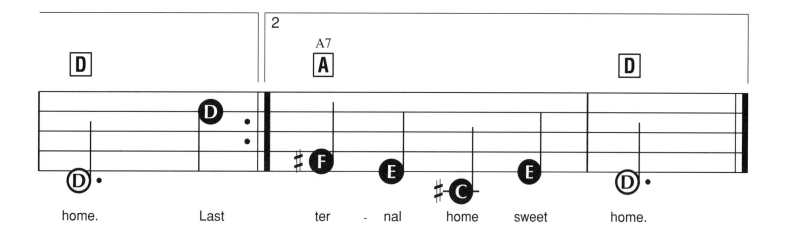

Jesus Is Calling

Registration 9
Rhythm: Country or Fox Trot

Words and Music by Hank Williams
and Charlie Monroe

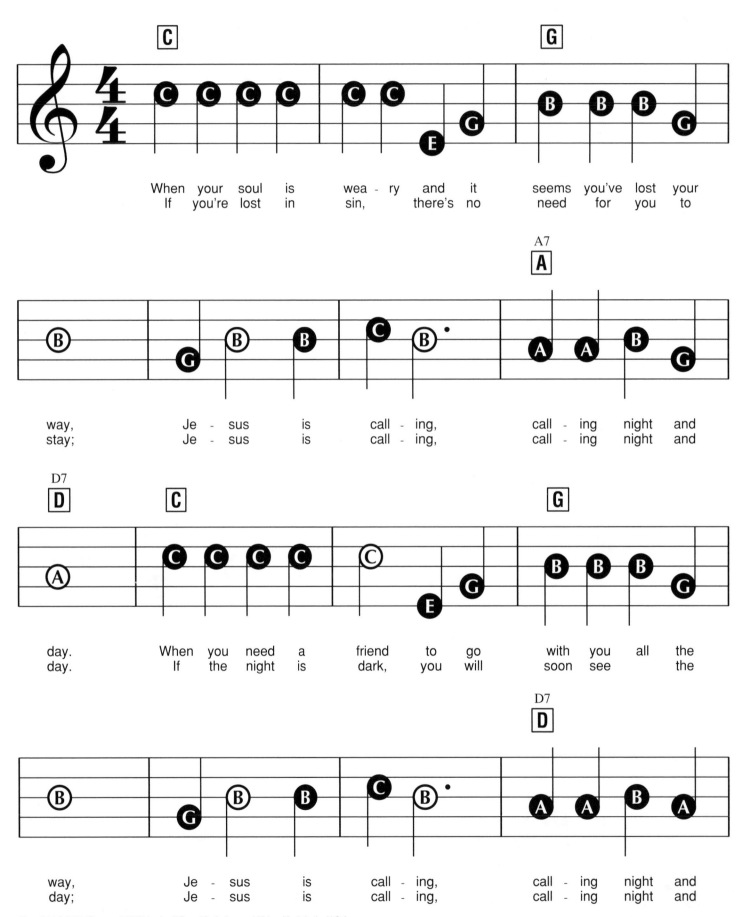

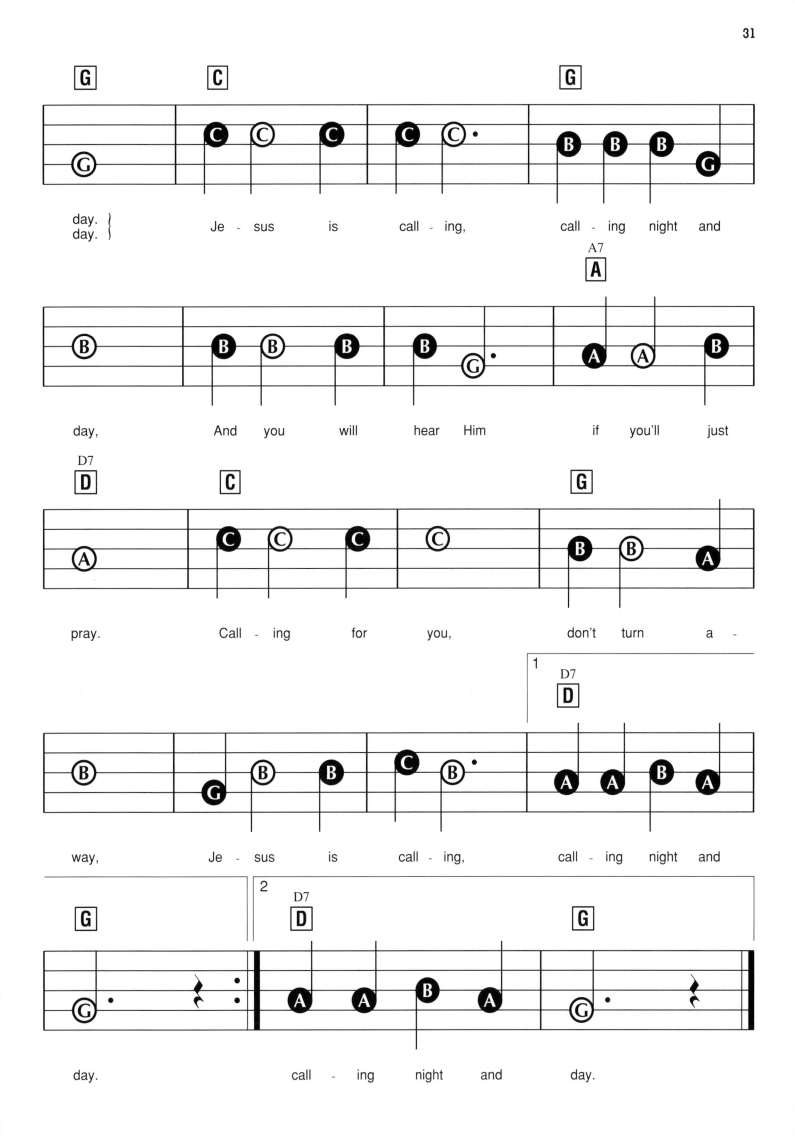

Jesus Remembered Me

Registration 4
Rhythm: Country or Fox Trot

Words and Music by
Hank Williams

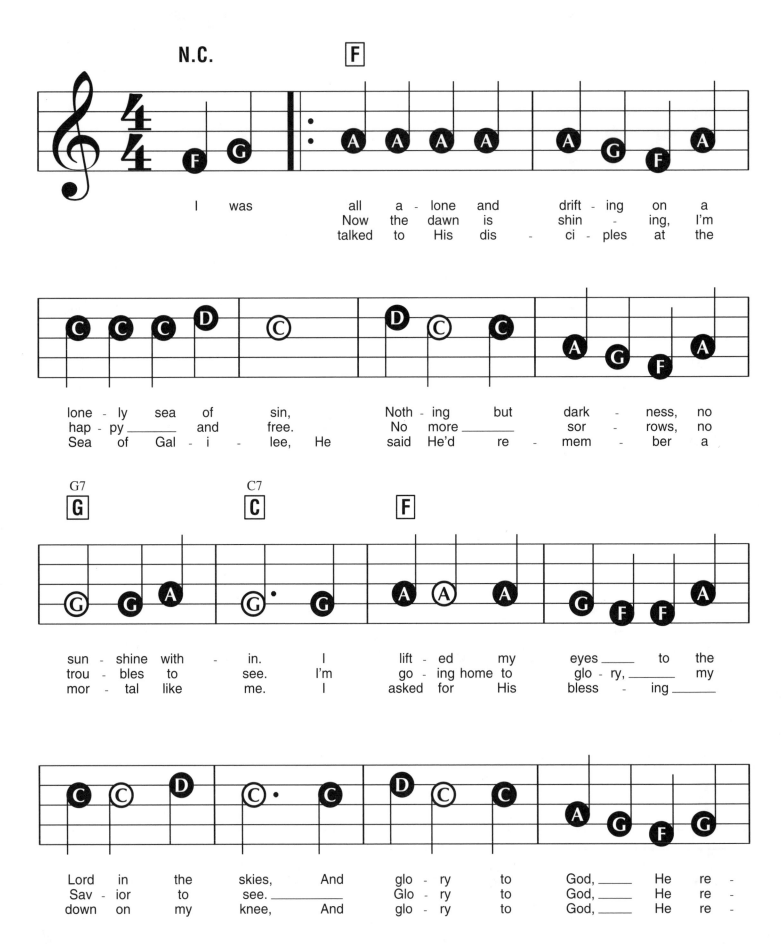

33

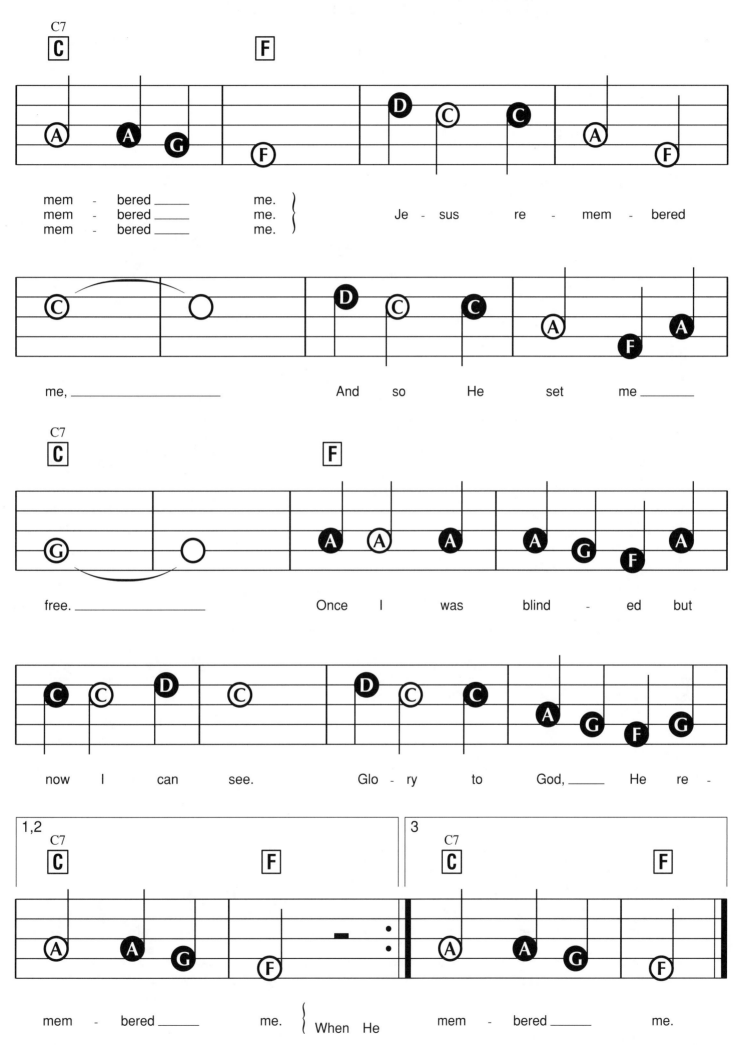

Message to My Mother

Registration 1
Rhythm: Country

Words and Music by
Hank Williams

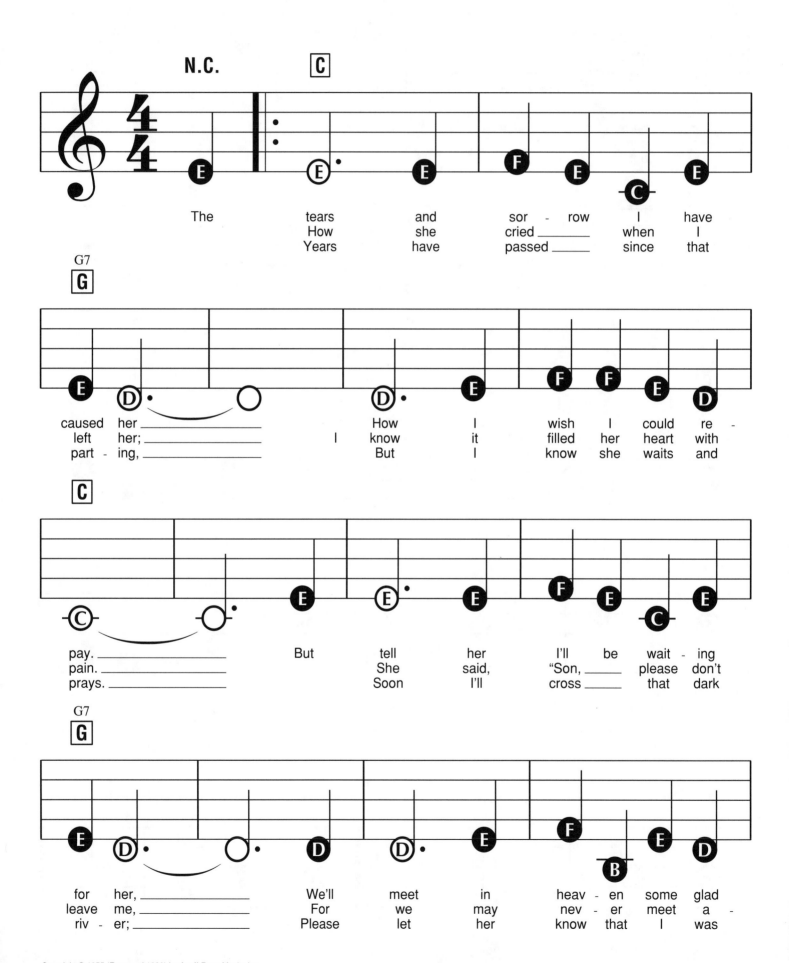

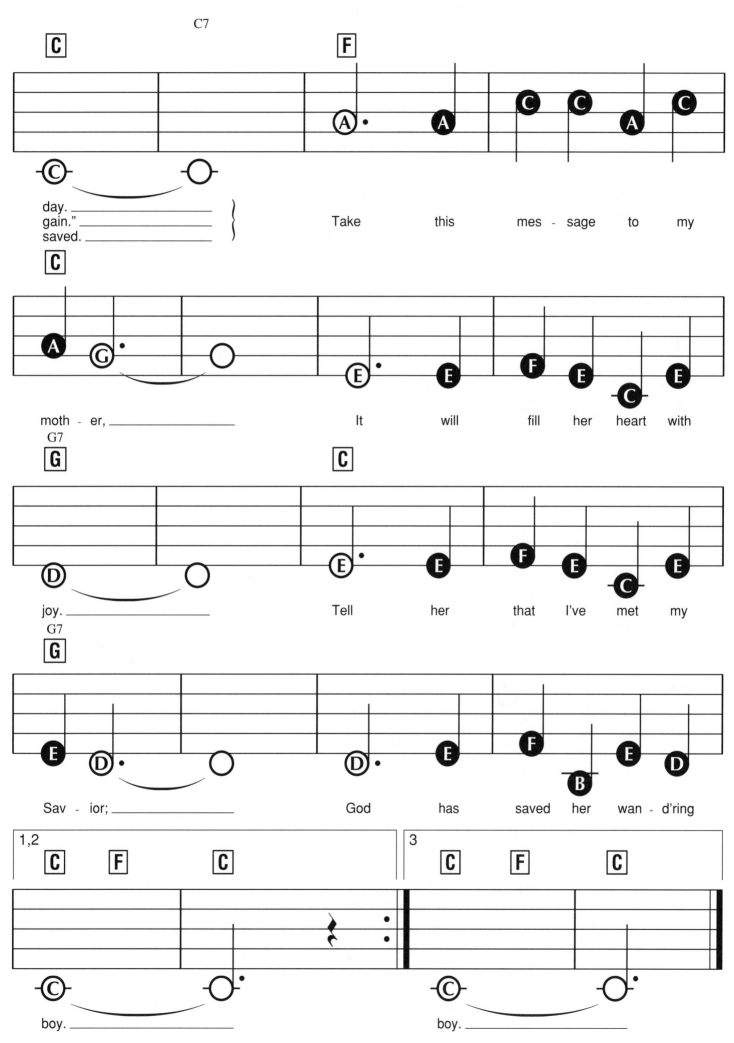

Mother Is Gone

Registration 10
Rhythm: Waltz

Words and Music by
Hank Williams

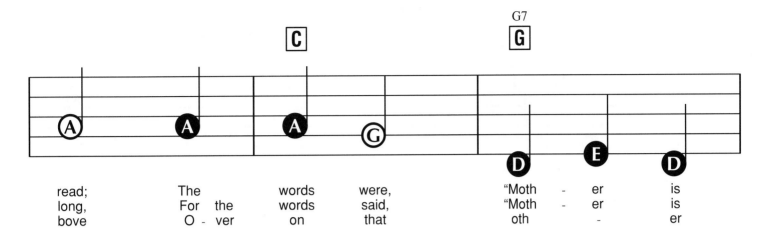

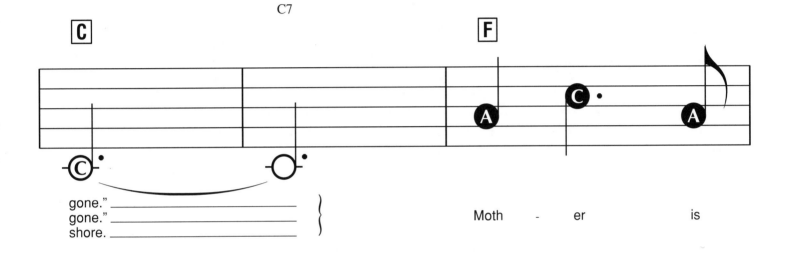

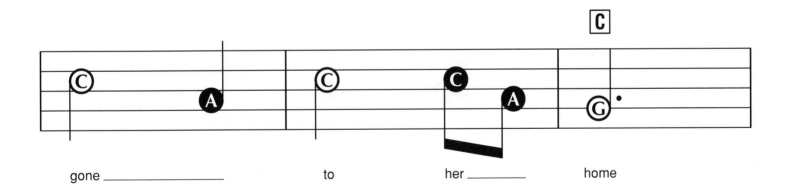

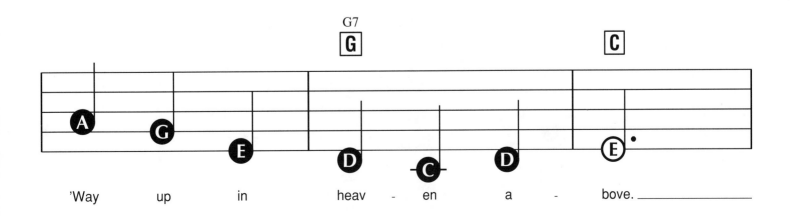

38

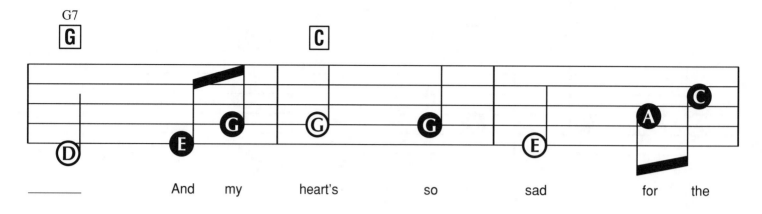

And my heart's so sad for the

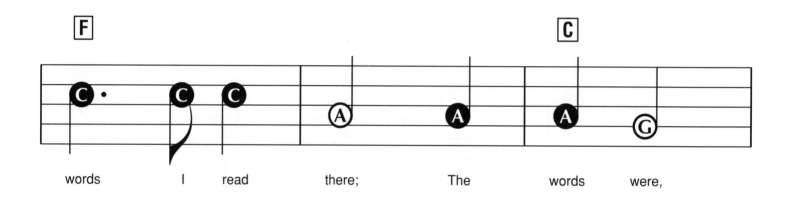

words I read there; The words were,

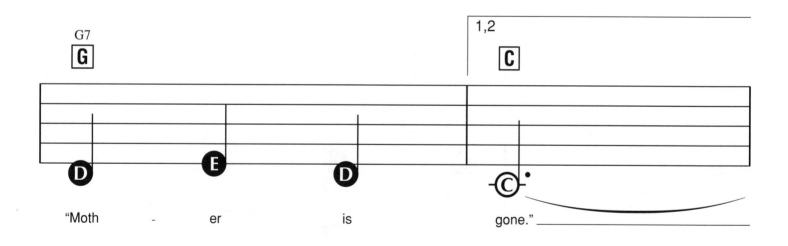

"Moth - er is gone."

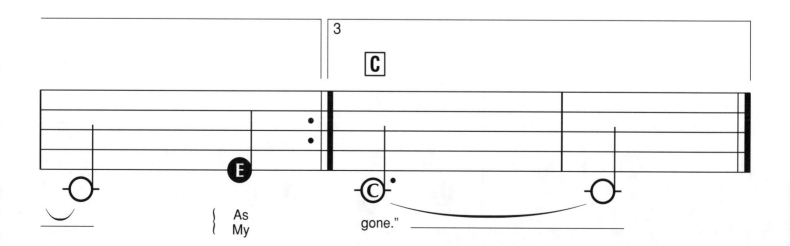

As
My gone."

(I'm Praying for the Day That)
Peace Will Come

Registration 7
Rhythm: Country

Words and Music by Hank Williams
and Pee Wee King

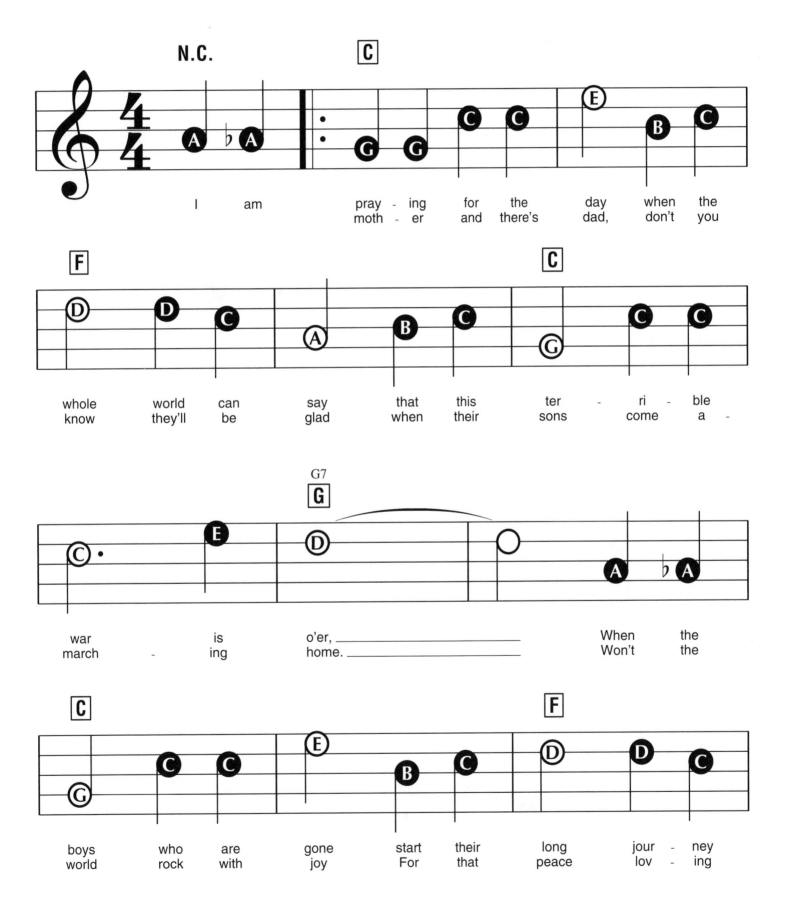

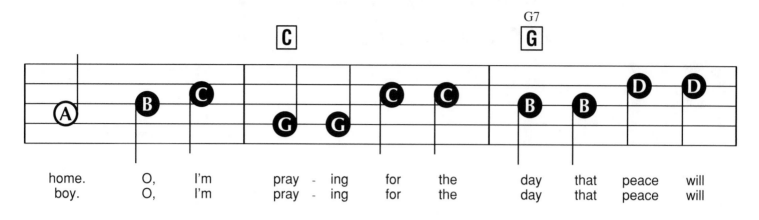

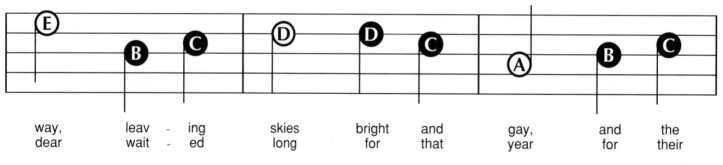

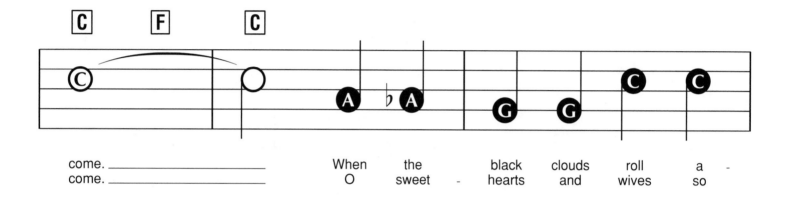

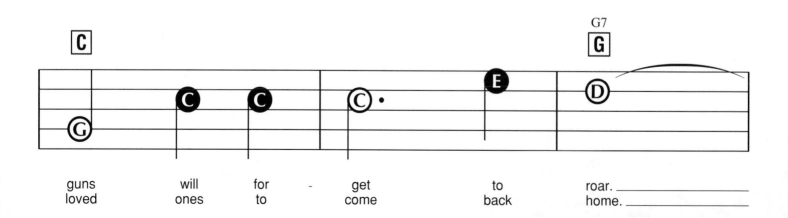

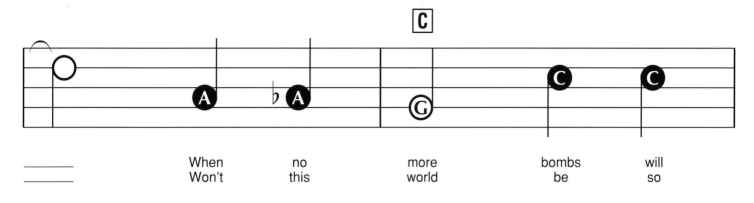

When no more bombs will
Won't this world be so

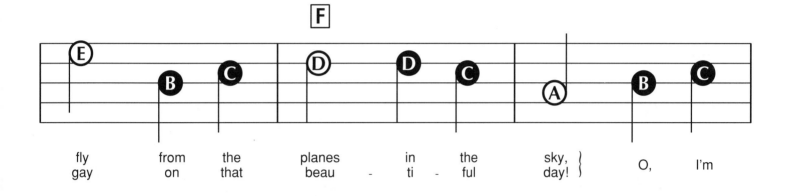

fly from the planes in the sky, } O, I'm
gay on that beau - ti - ful day!

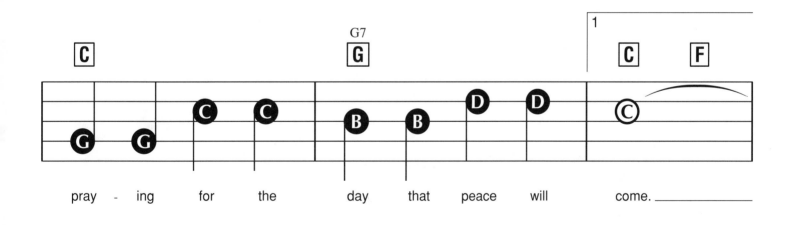

pray - ing for the day that peace will come. ___

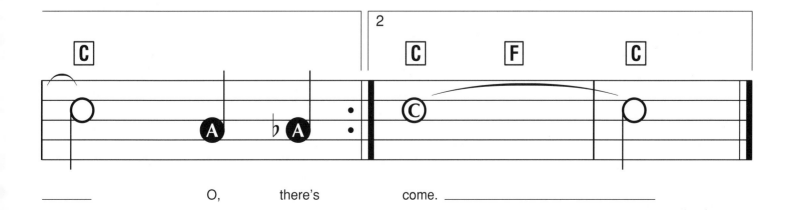

O, there's come. ___

Ready to Go Home

Registration 9
Rhythm: Country or Fox Trot

Words and Music by
Hank Williams

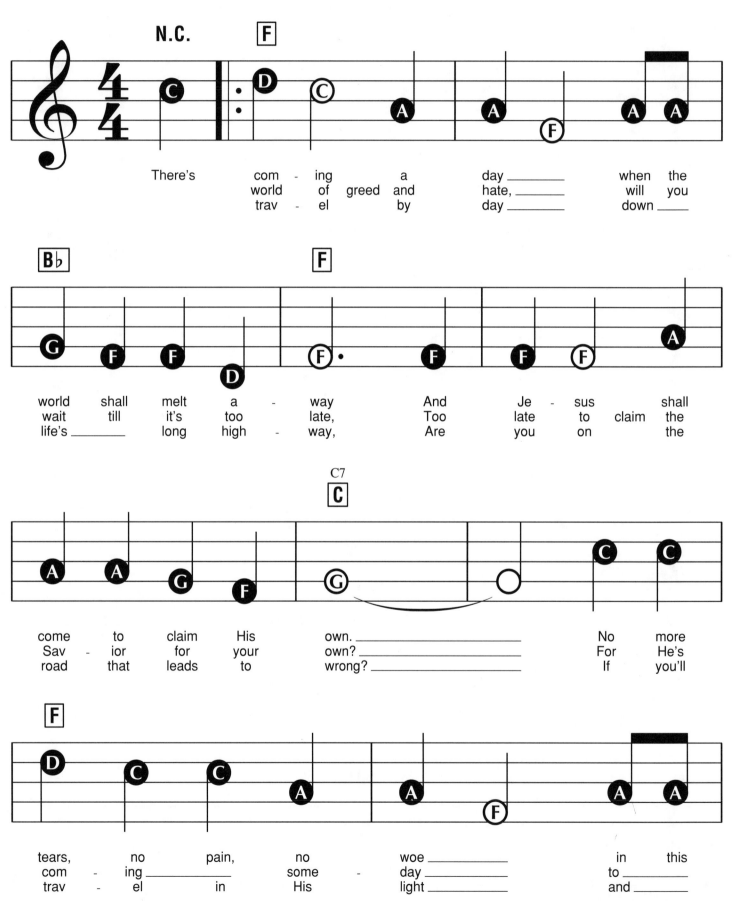

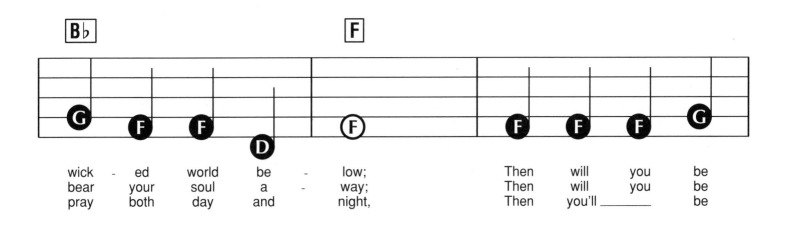

wick - ed world be - low;
bear your soul a - way;
pray both day and night,

Then will you be
Then will you be
Then you'll _____ be

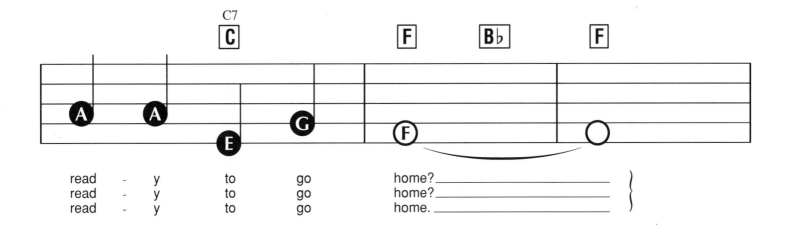

read - y to go home? _____
read - y to go home? _____
read - y to go home. _____

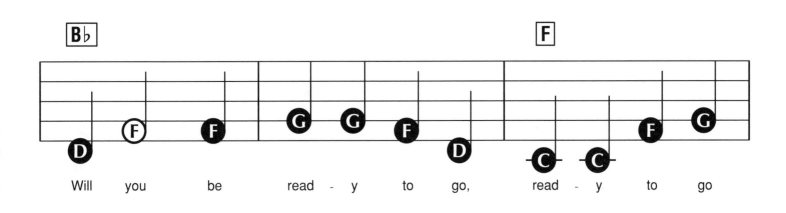

Will you be read - y to go, read - y to go

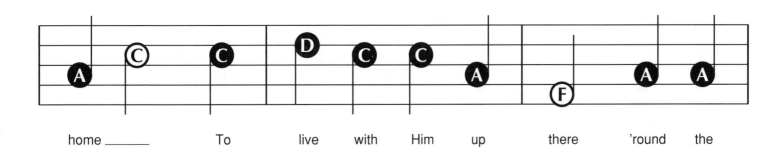

home _____ To live with Him up there 'round the

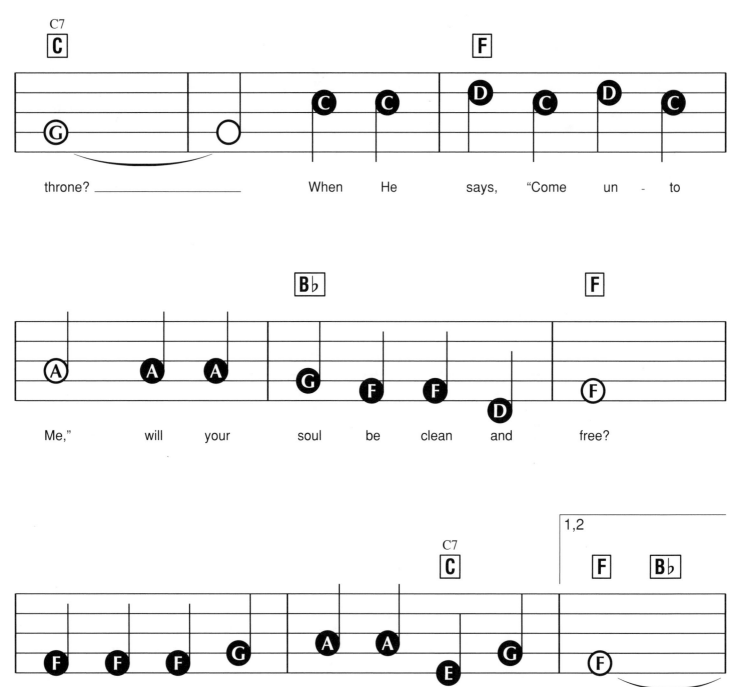

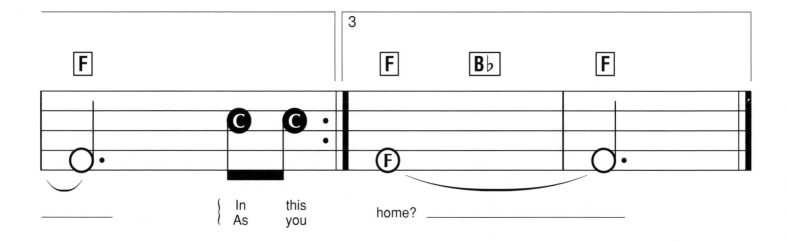

We're Getting Closer
to the Grave Each Day

Registration 1
Rhythm: Waltz

Words and Music by
Hank Williams

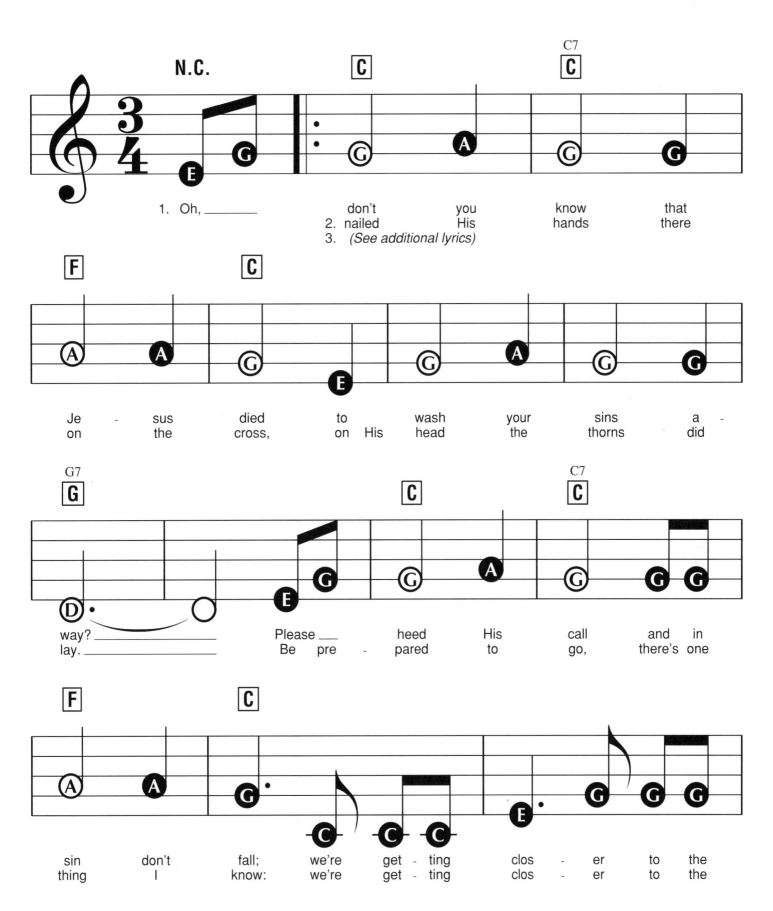

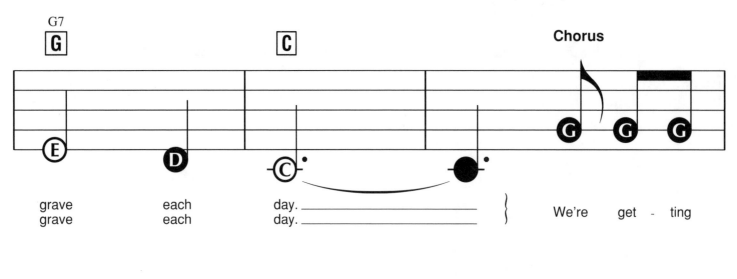

grave each day. _____ We're get - ting
grave each day. _____

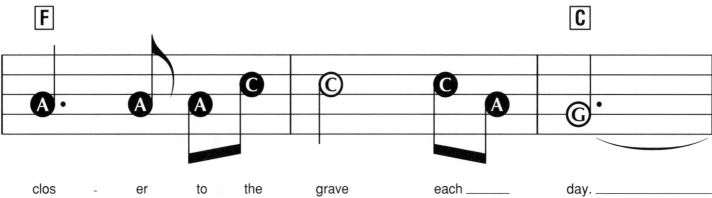

clos - er to the grave each _____ day. _____

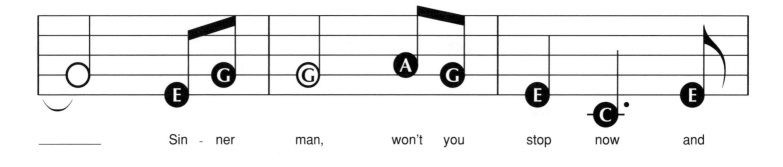

_____ Sin - ner man, won't you stop now and

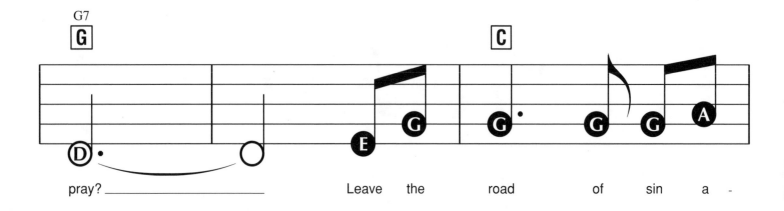

pray? _____ Leave the road of sin a -

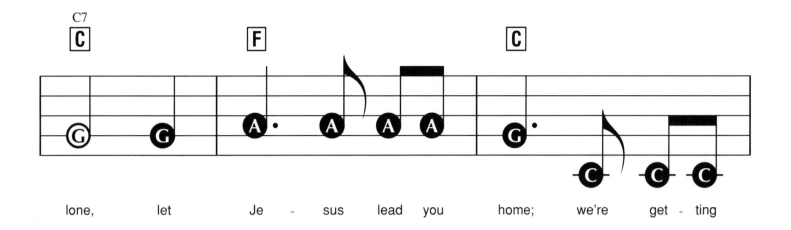

lone,   let   Je - sus   lead   you   home;   we're   get - ting

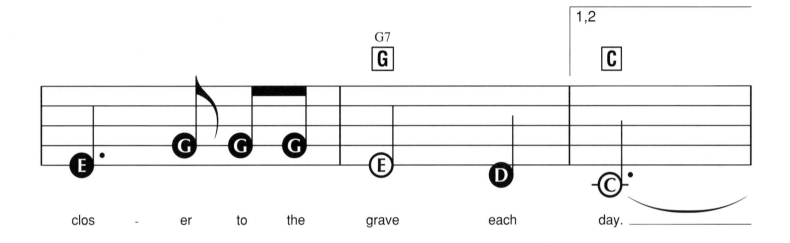

clos - er   to   the   grave   each   day. _____

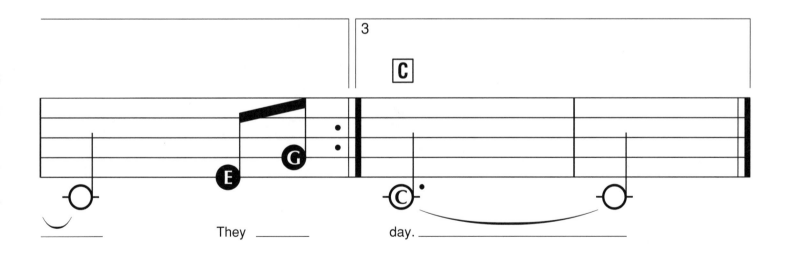

They _____ day. _____

Additional Lyrics

3. On the great judgment day when life's book is read,
   There'll be no time to pray.
   Learn to love and forgive while on earth you live;
   We're getting closer to the grave each day.
   Chorus

Wealth Won't Save Your Soul

Registration 3
Rhythm: Waltz

Words and Music by
Hank Williams

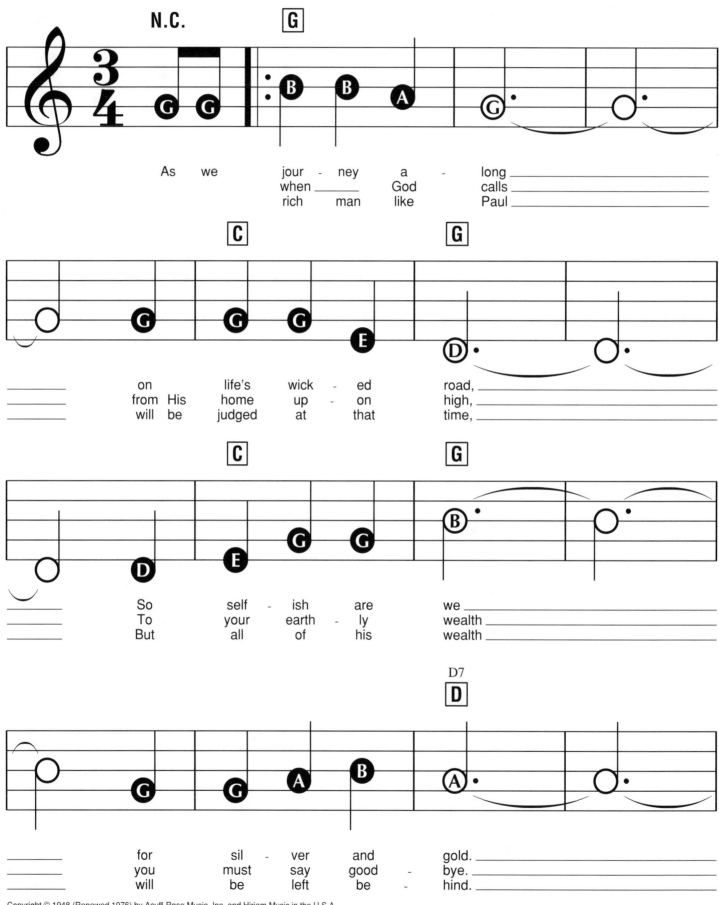

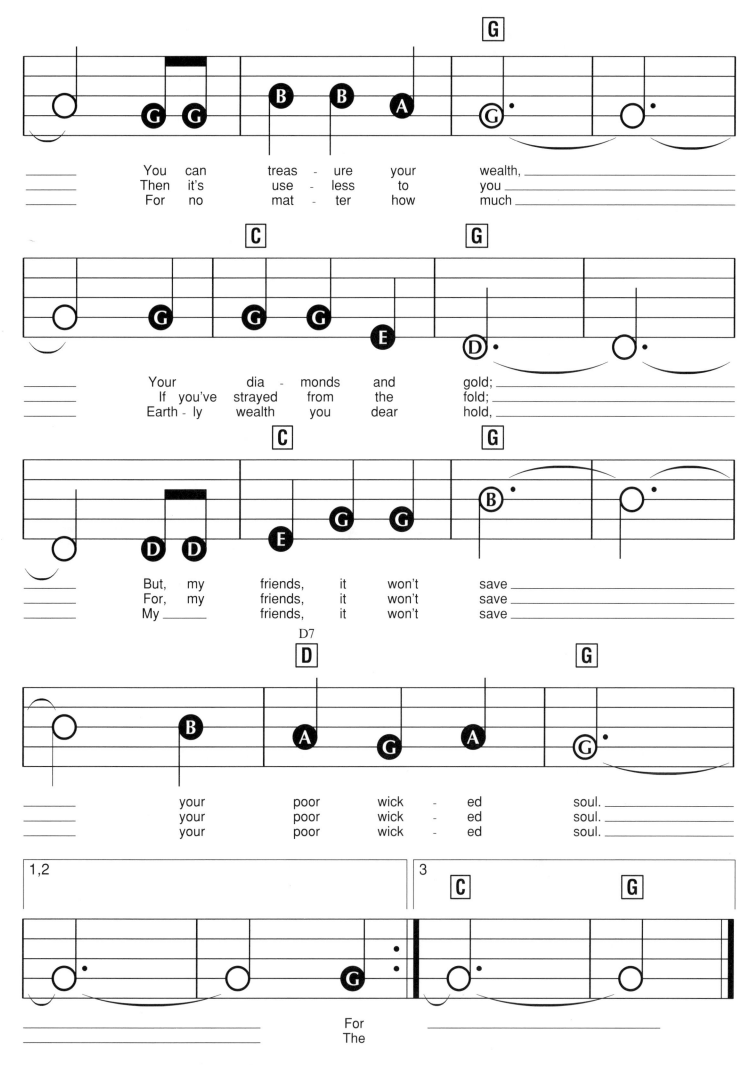

When God Comes and Gathers His Jewels

Registration 10
Rhythm: Waltz

Words and Music by
Hank Williams

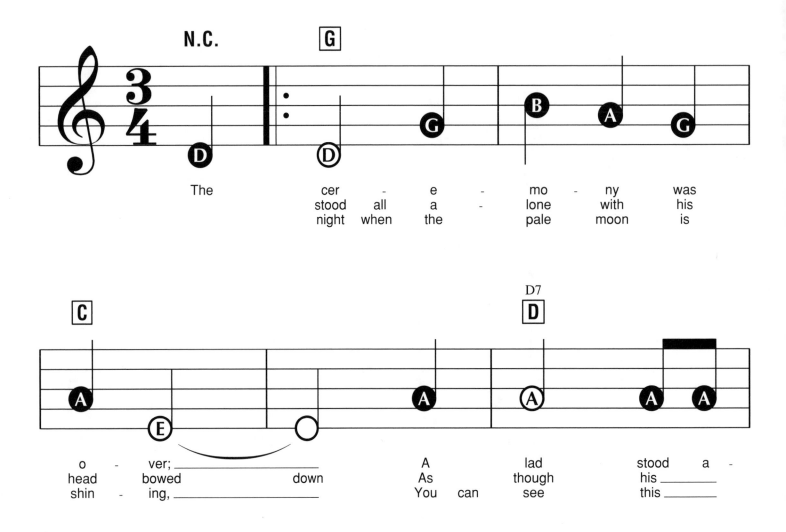

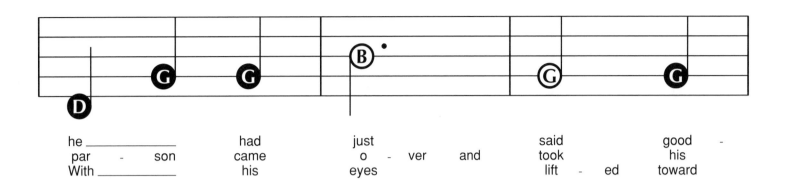

C

he _____ had just said good -
par - son had came o - ver and took his
With _____ his eyes lift - ed toward

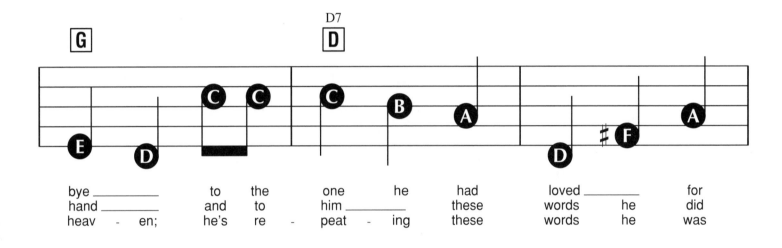

G   D7 D

bye _____ to the one he had loved _____ for
hand _____ to and him _____ these words he did
heav - en; he's re - peat - ing these words he was

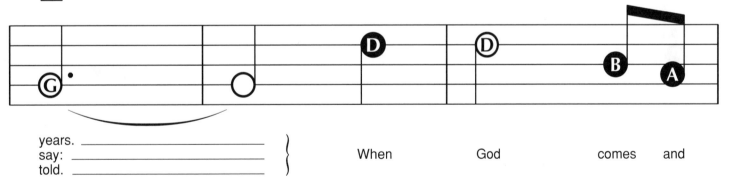

G

years. _____
say: _____
told. _____

When God comes and

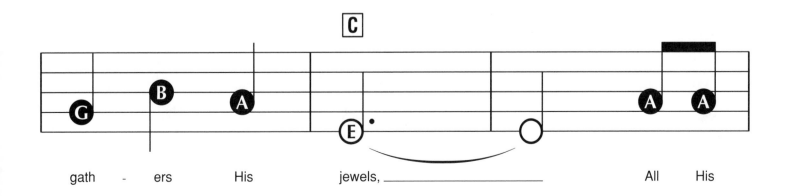

C

gath - ers His jewels, _____ All His

52

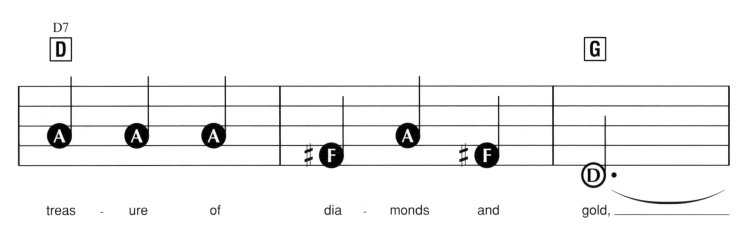

treas - ure of dia - monds and gold, _____

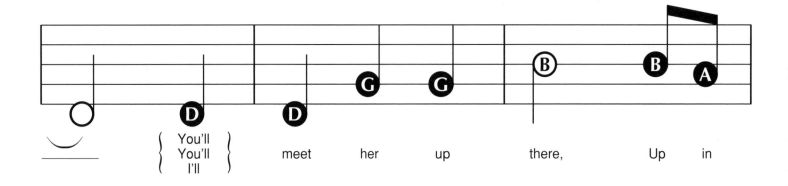

You'll
You'll   meet her up there,   Up in
I'll

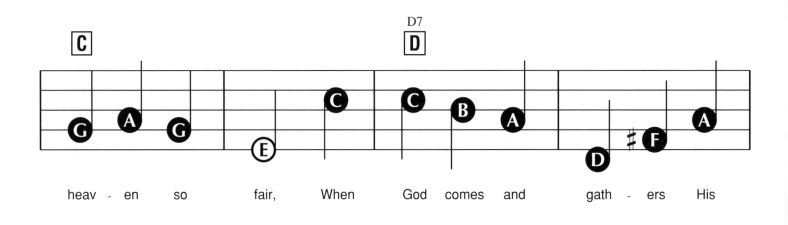

heav - en so fair, When God comes and gath - ers His

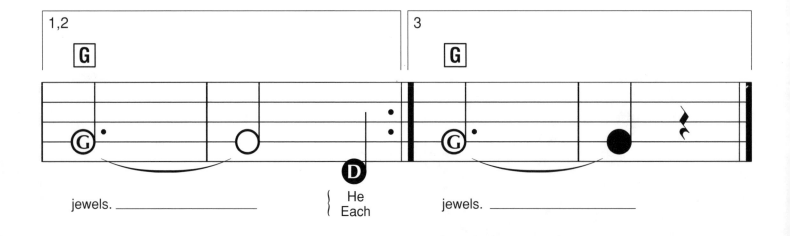

1,2   3

jewels. _____   He   jewels. _____
                         Each

When the Book of Life Is Read

Registration 9
Rhythm: Fox Trot

Words and Music by
Hank Williams

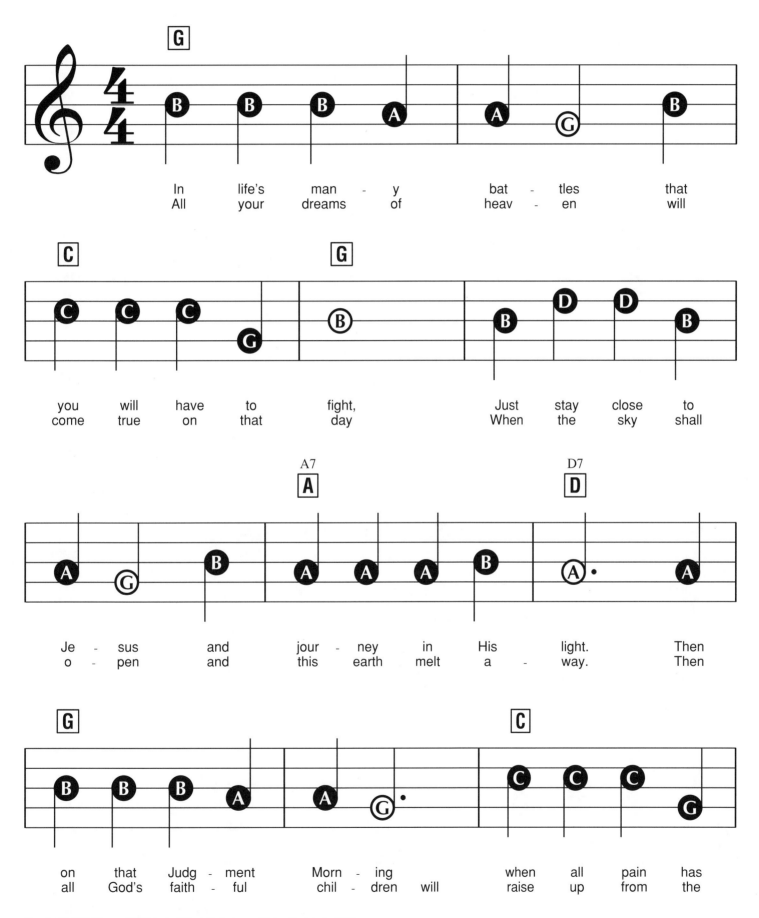

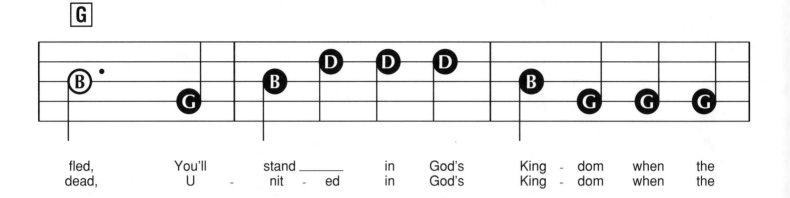

fled,   You'll   stand _____   in   God's   King - dom   when   the
dead,   U -   nit - ed   in   God's   King - dom   when   the

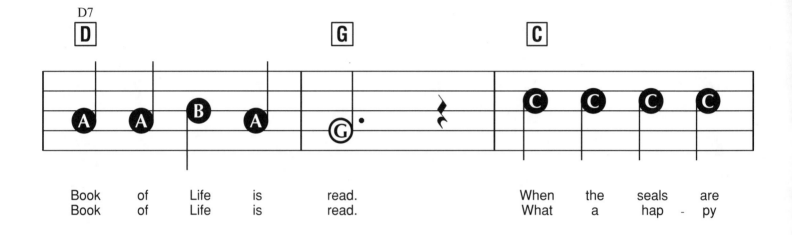

Book   of   Life   is   read.   When   the   seals   are
Book   of   Life   is   read.   What   a   hap - py

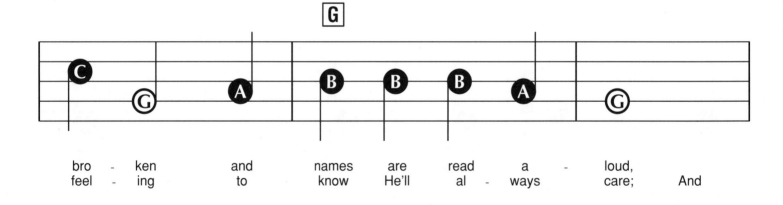

bro - ken   and   names   are   read   a -   loud,
feel - ing   to   know   He'll   al - ways   care;   And

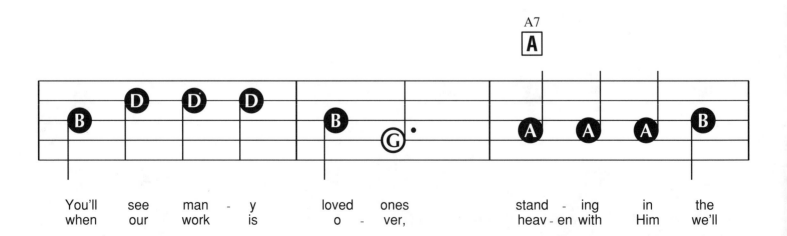

You'll   see   man - y   loved   ones   stand - ing   in   the
when   our   work   is   o - ver,   heav - en   with   Him   we'll

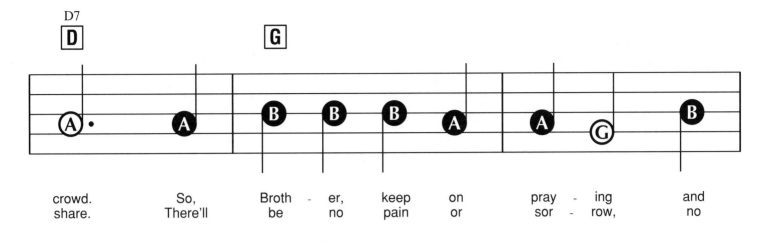

crowd.   So,   Broth - er,   keep   on   pray - ing   and
share.   There'll   be   no   pain   or   sor - row,   no

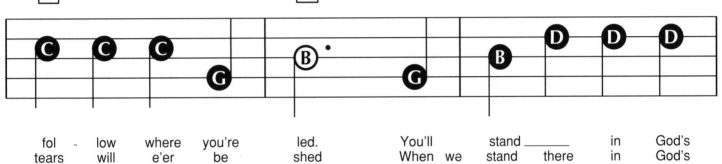

fol - low   where   you're   led.   You'll   stand _____ in God's
tears   will   e'er   be   shed   When   we   stand   there   in   God's

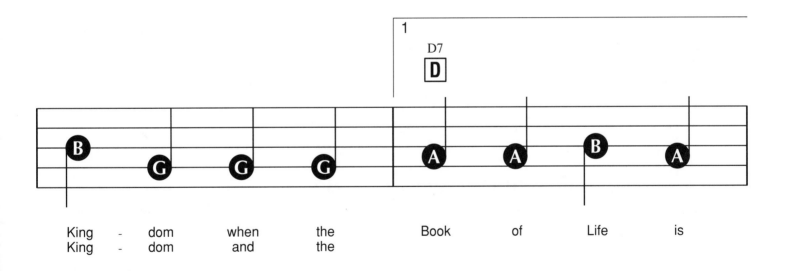

King - dom   when   the   Book   of   Life   is
King - dom   and   the   the

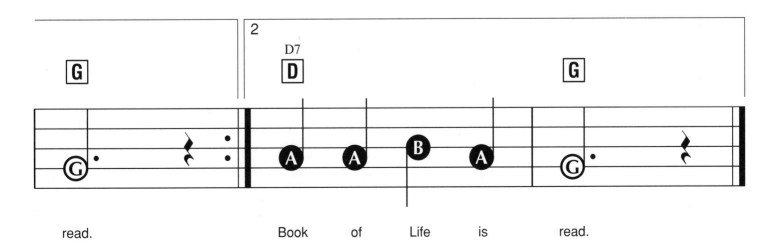

read.   Book   of   Life   is   read.

Registration Guide

- Match the Registration number on the song to the corresponding numbered category below. Select and activate an instrumental sound available on your instrument.

- Choose an automatic rhythm appropriate to the mood and style of the song. (Consult your Owner's Guide for proper operation of automatic rhythm features.)

- Adjust the tempo and volume controls to comfortable settings.

Registration

1	Flute, Pan Flute, Jazz Flute
2	Clarinet, Organ
3	Violin, Strings
4	Brass, Trumpet
5	Synth Ensemble, Accordion, Brass
6	Pipe Organ, Harpsichord
7	Jazz Organ, Vibraphone, Vibes, Electric Piano, Jazz Guitar
8	Piano, Electric Piano
9	Trumpet, Trombone, Clarinet, Saxophone, Oboe
10	Violin, Cello, Strings